張 義
Cheung Yee

Published on the occasion of The Art of Cheung Yee, organised by iPRECIATION

Published, designed and edited by
Author: Dr. Zhu Qi
iPRECIATION
T : (65) 6339 0678
F : (65) 6438 2080
1 FULLERTON SQUARE, #01-08
SINGAPORE 049178
IPRECIATION.COM

ISBN: 978-981-05-8716-1

張 義

Cheung Yee

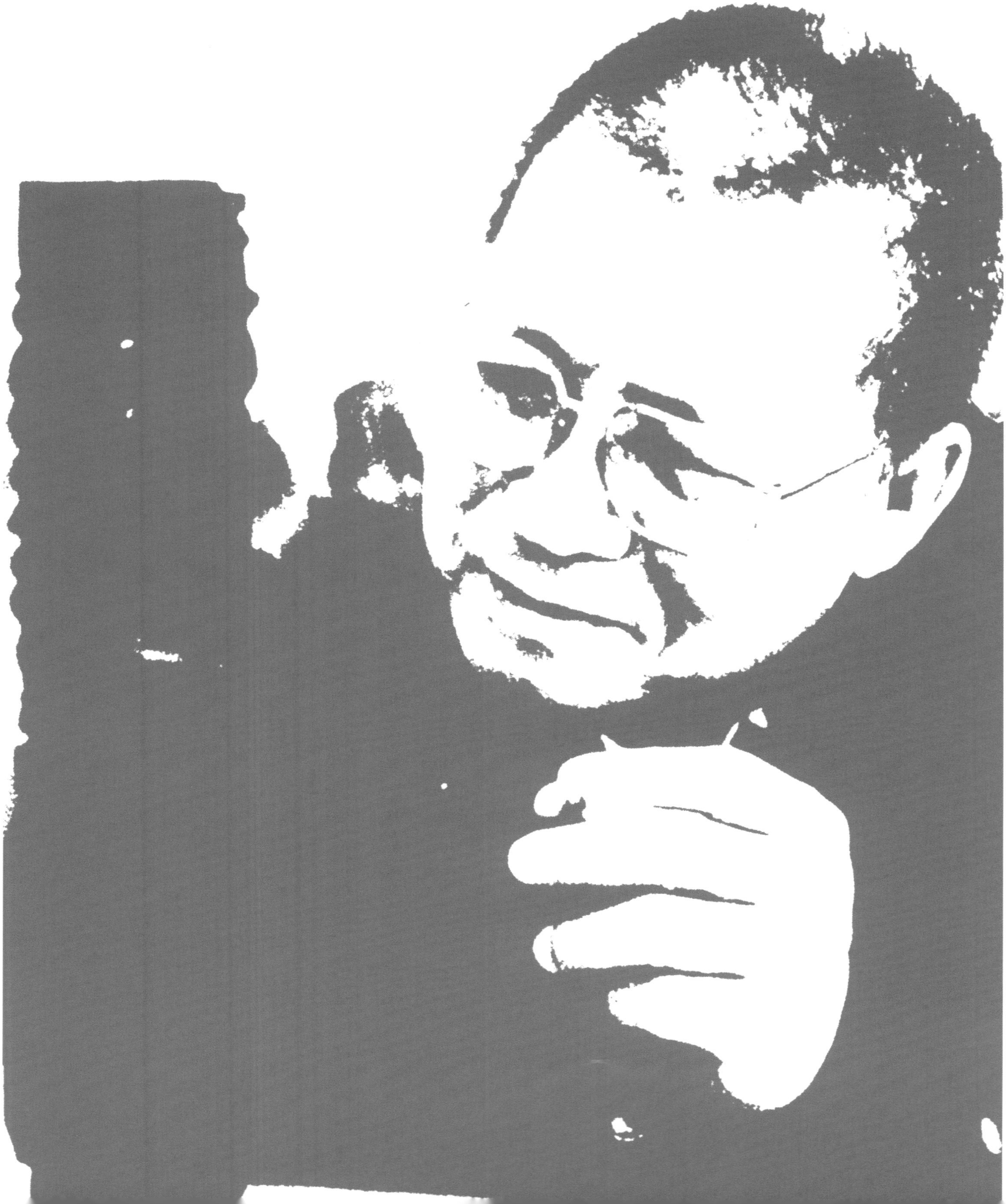

CONTENT

目錄

Message

Helina Chan

Knowing Cheung Yee since 1993, it is my firm belief that he is one of the most foundational pioneers of the modern movement in Chinese sculpture – not simply in the redesigning of sculptural form, but also in reviving the great artistic, historical, and philosophical traditions of China within his works.

As a master sculptor, Cheung Yee is an exemplary craftsman. His immense skill and dedication to the creation of his art causes each work to be unique in its own right. Each creation is distinctive and beautiful, carrying a message of historical or philosophical significance.

Cheung Yee was made a Member of the British Empire in 1979, a rare honour for a Chinese artist from Hong Kong. This proved beyond all doubt that not only was Cheung Yee making a vast impact through the unusual cultural language of his modern, yet historically inspired works, he was also being recognised beyond his own industry for his contributions in pioneering this school.

In the 1980s and 1990s, his work continued to evolve and expand with increasing degrees of sophistication and complexity. What we see today is the result of decades of unceasing perseverance to creating an outstanding legacy for the world of Chinese art.

Despite the dominance of modern Western artists, Cheung Yee has managed to hold his own with exceptional modernist works, while maintaining the creation of a distinctively Chinese artistic experience as his primary goal. Future generations of contemporary artists will look towards significant forebears such as Cheung Yee for inspiration in retaining their Chinese identity within an increasingly cosmopolitan artistic context.

This monograph is a catalogue of his works from the 1964 to 2007.

I hope you enjoy his captivating works!

序言

陳淑娟

我自1993年以來便認識張義。我深信他是為中華現代雕塑奠下最根本基礎的先驅人物之一。他的功績不僅在於改造雕塑藝術形式，更在於通過作品振興中國偉大的藝術、歷史與哲學傳統。

作為一位雕塑大師，張義在藝術工作上堪作楷模。他在創作上灌注的高超技藝以及大量心血，使得每一件作品都自成一格。他的傑作無不各具特色，瑰奇動人，而且寄寓著歷史或哲學奧義。

張義在1979年獲得了香港華族藝術家當中極為罕見的一項榮譽—大英帝國勛章（MBE）。這毫無疑問証明了一點：張義取諸歷史而又富有現代氣息的作品，不僅以其非一般的文化語言帶來了重大的沖擊，也因為開創此類藝術之功而受到了藝術界以外的肯定。

他的作品在1980及90年代一直演變擴展，其精妙與復雜性都日漸提升。我們今日所見，實為張義為了給世人留下傑出的中華藝術遺產，數十年來耕耘不懈的成果。

盡管世界藝壇多以西方現代藝術家為尊，張義還是一面主要堅持創造有中華特色的藝術體驗，一面憑極為出色的現代主義作品保有一定的地位。當代藝術界的後來者必將有感於像張義這樣功高力偉的前輩們，在國際色彩越來越濃的藝術背景中力求保留自己的華族身份認同。

本著作為張義作品集，載錄的是他從1964年到2007年的作品。

願您遨游在他引人入勝的藝術天地裡，深得其樂！

Constancy and Adaptations in Cheung Yee's Sculptures

Dr. Zhu Qi

The emergence of modern art trends in Hong Kong began from the late 1950s onwards when the territory's economy was taking off rapidly, ideology attenuating and the society drifting towards Westernisation. Painters of both the traditional Chinese and Western style (including Lui Shou Kwan, Kwong Yeu Ting and Pak Lin) formed the Hong Kong Artists Association in 1957, blazing new paths for the development of art in Hong Kong. Inspired by the modern art pioneers of Hong Kong and Taiwan, the Society of Modern Literature and Fine Arts and the Chung Yuen Art Society were subsequently established by a group of young artists native to Hong Kong and returning from their studies in Taiwan. In their artistic practice, these organisations did more than flaunting a modernist style. They explicitly set forth "a direction of development that was to be Hong Kong's, Oriental and Chinese" (Wucius Wong, "A View of Hong Kong's Art Based on A Few Hong Kong Art Societies", in *An Exhibition on the History of Art Groups in Hong Kong* (Hong Kong: Executive Committee for *An Exhibition on the History of Art Groups in Hong Kong*, 1993)). Thus driven by one wave after another, modern art in Hong Kong managed to break through the perennial dominance of traditional art. With the support of government agencies, it quickly rose to become the mainstream in the local art scene.

Cheung Yee is a representative figure in the history of Hong Kong's modern art. His sculptures, along with those of Van Lau, the Chinese ink paintings of Lui Shou Kwan, Wucius Wong, Irene Chou and Chu Hing Wah, as well as the Western paintings of Luis Chan, Pak Lin, Kwong Yeu Ting, Jackson Yu Shao Tseng, Hon Chi Fun and Gaylord Chan constitute a stylistically diverse body of works that shapes the basic outlook of Hong Kong's modern art.

Born to a family of ceramists in Guangzhou, Cheung Yee has loved craftwork ever since childhood. He once came under Ting Yen Yung's tutelage during his adolescent years at Tak Ming Middle School. In 1954, Cheung enrolled in the Art Department of the Taiwan Normal University, where he focused on studying traditional Chinese realistic painting and seal carving. He worked in the former discipline after graduating and returning to Hong Kong in 1958, only to participate in the modern art movement shortly after, in which he became one of the founding members of two groups - the Society of Modern Literature and Fine Arts, and the Chung Yuen Art Society. It was a shift in Cheung Yee's conception of art and his discontent with Chinese artists' underachievement in the domain of sculpture (in spite of their significant success in painting worldwide and of the greatness attained by Chinese sculptures in ancient times) that motivated him to turn to creating sculptures with the hope of achieving some kind of breakthrough ("Recreating the Mystique of Ancient Tiles in Carving – Li Xianwen's Interview of Cheung Yee", collated by Zhang Jianlong and published in *Hsiung Shih Art Monthly*, August 1985).

3D artistic space lends greater liberty to Cheung's vigorous creativity. By the great rivers of Chinese civilisation carved out by his ancestors, he treads upstream, all the while being nourished and inspired thereby. As an admirer of the *I Ching*, Cheung is able to skillfully apply the ways of constancy and adaptation in its ancient philosophy to his own artistic practice. He is adept at achieving canonicity amidst variations and transformations amidst constants through substitutions of both materials and themes. In this manner, Cheung has been able to frequently generate a new look for his art, making valuable contributions to Hong

張義雕塑的“經”與“權”

朱琦博士

50年代後期起，香港經濟快速發展，意識形態逐漸淡薄，社會風尚趨於西化，現代藝術思潮開始顯露端倪。當時，呂壽琨、鄺耀鼎、白連等中西畫家率先於1957年成立了“香港藝術家協會”，為香港藝術的發展開辟了新的路徑。隨後，一批香港本地和從台灣留學歸來的藝術青年，在港台現代藝術先驅的激勵下，又相繼成立了“現代文學美術協會”和“中元畫會”。這些畫會在創作上除了標舉現代風格外，還明確提出了“香港、東方、中國的發展路向”（王無邪：“從香港幾個畫會看香港藝術”，見《香港美術團體歷史展覽》，香港美術團體歷史展覽執委會出版，1993年）。香港的現代藝術在這一波波浪潮的推動下，打破了長期以來傳統藝術一統天下的局面，並在官方機構的支持下，一躍而為當地藝壇的主流。

在香港現代藝術的發展過程中，張義是一位頗具代表性的人物。他與文樓的雕塑，呂壽琨、王無邪、周綠雲、朱興華等人的水墨畫，以及陳福善、白蓮、鄺耀鼎、尤紹曾、韓志勛、陳餘生等人的西畫，風格各異，但又共同構成了香港現代藝術的基本面貌。

張義出生於廣州的一個陶瓷業者家庭，從小喜愛手工勞作。少年時代在德明中學就讀時，曾得到過丁衍庸的指導。1954年考入台灣師范大學藝術系，重點學習傳統工筆畫和篆刻。1958年畢業後返港，從事工筆畫創作，不久又投入現代藝術運動，成為“現代文學美術協會”和“中元畫會”的創會會員。藝術觀念的轉變，加上有感於華人在國際畫壇已取得一定成就，惟在雕塑領域尚無建樹，與中國古代輝煌的雕塑成就極不相稱，張義於是轉而從事雕塑創作，以期在這方面有所突破（張建隆整理：“雕出瓦古的幽秘—李賢文訪張義”，見《雄獅美術》，1985年8月）。

三維的藝術空間，讓創造力旺盛的張義有了更大的施展余地。他沿著祖先開鑿的中華文明大河溯流而上，不斷從中吸取靈感和養分。由於尊崇周易學說，張義將其中的經權之道，巧妙地運用於自己的創作實踐中。他善於通過材料和題材的變換，在“易”中謀“經”、於不變中求變，從而使自己的創作風貌，時常展現出柳暗花明又一村的景象，為香港藝壇的卓越多姿帶來了寶貴的貢獻。

Kong's remarkable and variegated art scene.

The development of Cheung Yee's art may be delineated by the following stages:

I. Inception of a Personal Style

In the late 1950s, Cheung Yee embarked on his ambitious journey in sculptural art as he started working with pieces of metal, wood and stone. Immensely inspired by the work of the British sculptor Henry Moore, he developed a profound interest in primitive art and ancient Chinese carvings. Works like the stone sculpture *Mother and Child* (1958) show early signs of his eventual style with the intriguing formation of images in concordance with the underlying materials.

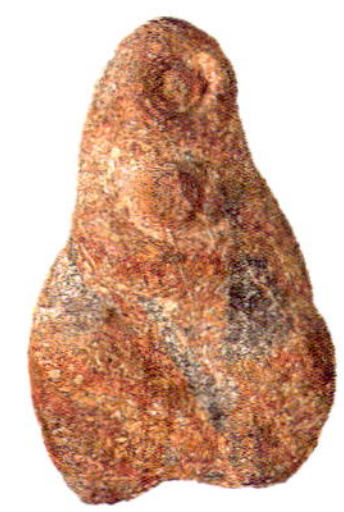

Mother & Child 母子, *Granite, H: 22 cm, 1958*

By the early 1960s, Cheung was producing a great number of bronze reliefs and wooden simulacra of bronzes inscribed with ancient Chinese writings and decorative motifs. The bronze relief *Four Spirits* (which was selected for the Hong Kong City Hall Museum and Art Gallery's 1962 Hong Kong Art Today exhibition), for instance, was modelled after ancient Chinese scripts in conjunction with the use of *tao-tie* motifs found on archaic bronzes, as well as that of the images of mythological beasts. A certain fascination with rubbings of tortoise shell / bone oracle inscriptions is also evident in Cheung's bronze reliefs, in which he often shaped the form of a tortoise shell on thin pieces of bronze that were subsequently inscribed with oracle pictographs. One such example is *Immortality* (1962), which was modelled after rubbings of oracle pictographs. Nevertheless, at this stage, Cheung's interest in the form of the tortoise shell was still limited to the lines of the inscriptions thereon. He had yet to pay great attention to tortoise shells *per se*, but merely viewed them as surfaces for the oracle inscriptions. In a joint exhibition with Lin Zhenhui in 1963, Cheung showcased another group of his ancient-looking works created in this period – wooden simulacra of bronzes. Not only were these sculptures endowed with an archaic flavour via the hues of bronze and verdigris on their surfaces, the grain and cracks of the wood itself were not concealed in any way, resulting in a natural allure that shines through the ancient appearance. In addition to simulacra of bronzes, Cheung also made many wooden sculptures in emulation of primitive totems and pottery. These bird-like, serpentine and humanoid forms were inscribed with oracle pictographs and then painted in verdigris to imbue them with a primeval tension that is both pristine and mystical.

These quasi-bronze, quasi-pottery and quasi-wooden simulacra of antique artefacts were directly inspired by Chinese culture of the distant past. To this, the artist had added his own romantic imagination and modern artistic expression to achieve special aesthetic effects. When an exhibition of Cheung Yee's recent works was held at the Hong Kong City Hall Museum and Art Gallery in 1964 to display the fruits of his artistic endeavours in a more comprehensive fashion, it was clear that Cheung had basically established by then the direction of his artistic development with respect to both theme and mode of expression.

II. "Tortoise Shell" Period

分析張義的藝術歷程，約略可歸納為以下幾個階段：

一、風格初創時期

50年代末，張義以金屬片、木頭和石頭為材料，開始了他雄心勃勃的雕塑藝術之旅。他從英國雕塑家亨利•摩爾的作品中獲得了很大啟示，對原始藝術和中國古代雕刻產生了濃厚的興趣，所作如石雕《母子》（1958），因材造像，耐人尋味，初步顯露出他的雕塑風格端倪。

60年代初，張義創作了大量帶有中國古代文字和裝飾符號的青銅浮雕和仿青銅器的木雕。入選1962年香港大會堂博物美術館“今日香港藝術”展的銅浮雕《四靈》，即以中國古文字為造型，並採用了古代青銅器上的饕餮紋和神話異獸形象。他在青銅浮雕創作上，還對甲骨文拓片情有獨鐘，經常在薄銅片上敲出龜板的外形，再刻上甲骨文。例如，銅浮雕《永生》（1962），便是以甲骨文拓片為藍本而完成的。不過，張義此時對於龜甲造型的興趣，還只限於所刻文字的線條，對龜甲本身未予重視，僅將其視為負載甲骨文的平面。1963年，張義在與林鎮輝的聯展中，又展出了他於同一時期創作的形態古拙的仿青銅器木雕，這些木雕的表面涂了古銅色和銅綠色，古器味十足，但木頭本身的紋理和裂痕仍保留著，不作任何掩飾，古意中帶有自然之趣。除了模仿青銅器，張義也創作了大量模仿原始圖騰和陶器的木雕，並把甲骨文刻在這些鳥形、蛇形、人形的木雕上，再涂以銅綠色，使之具有古朴而神秘的原始張力。

張義的這些似銅非銅、似陶非陶、似木非木的仿古雕刻，直接從中國遠古文化中吸取營養，並結合個人浪漫的想象，以現代藝術手法加以表現，具有特殊的審美效果。1964年，香港大會堂美術館為其舉辦了“張義近作展”，較全面地展示了他這一時期的創作成果，反映出他在題材和表現形式上已基本確立了自己的藝術發展方向。

二、“龜甲”時期

1965年，張義在國際教育學院獎學金的資助下赴歐美作藝術交

In 1965, Cheung Yee headed for Europe and the USA for an artistic exchange under an International Education Institute scholarship. The West was to influence him with pop art and neo-Dadaism. Upon returning to Hong Kong, he experienced a significant breakthrough when he experimented with art produced with ready-made objects. Nevertheless, he had to forgo such attempts in the end as such popular art had its origin in Western consumerist society and was a world apart from his cultural roots.

In the following year, the exploring artist began to turn his attention once again to the locus of his passion prior to the USA trip - the form of the tortoise shell. It was to take on new manifestations time and again, and to become a major theme in Cheung's art. Starting off with 2D rubbings of oracle pictographs, Cheung went on to divinatory tortoise shell reliefs, and then to fully 3D figures of tortoise shells, conceptually enriched with other ancient mythological imageries. By this stage, the tortoise shell was no longer a mere shamanistic item for the purpose of divination, but a veritable carrier of Chinese culture and mysterious stories of high antiquity (Zhao Jincheng, "Cheung Yee's Archetropic Art", in *Cheung Yee's Sculptures* (Hong Kong: Hong Kong Urban Council, 1993)).

In 1968, Cheung Yee's wooden relief *Genesis* was displayed in the Chung Yuen Art Society's 5th exhibition. It was one of his most successful tortoise shell-based artwork. Consisting of 12 differently rendered tortoise shell reliefs, it features a square on the outside with a large circle within. The tortoise shells inside the circle are more richly carved, covered with irregular barnacles and holes not unlike what one might see through a microscope. In stark contrast, the shells outside of the circle look simple and unadorned. Evident here is an Oriental philosophical outlook characterised by "a square on the outside and a circle inside".

Another epitome of the tortoise shell theme would be the wooden sculpture *Four Spirits*. When Cheung worked on such pieces, he employed openwork techniques on the spaces between the tortoise shells. As for the decorative motifs on every shell – be they barnacles, vaginal patterns, wormholes or abstract forms – he would also apply piercings of various depths and curvatures, resulting in works with an air of natural simplicity as well as totem-like augustness and sombreness.

In the late 1960s, Cheung Yee also created a batch of cast bronze tortoise-shaped mini-sculptures, which further expanded the diversity of his tortoise shell oeuvre.

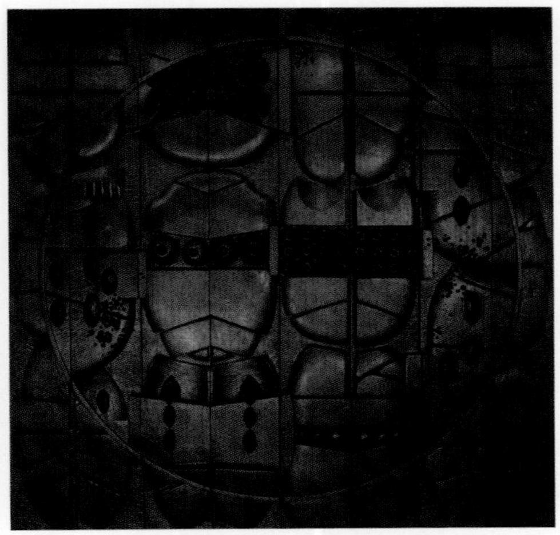

Genesis 原, Wood, 244 x 244 cm, 1968

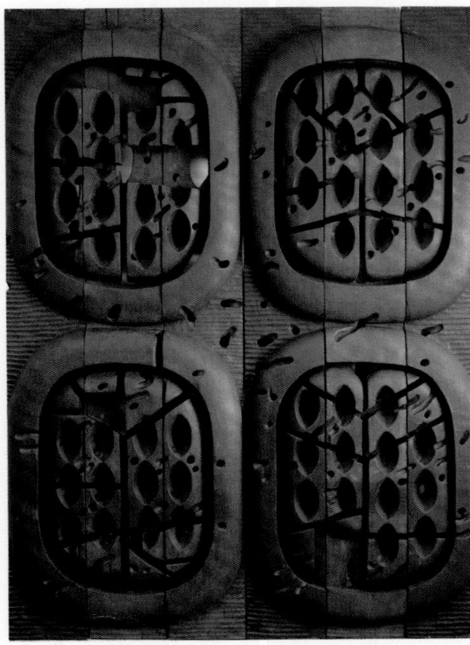

Four Spirits 四靈, Wood, 264 x 183 cm, 1975

流，在那裡接受了波普藝術以及新達達主義的影響。回港後，他嘗試利用現成品進行創作，試圖在藝術上有較大的突破。然而，這種源於西方消費社會的流行藝術，與他的文化根源相去甚遠，最終不得不放棄。

翌年開始，張義幾經探索，興趣又回到了留美前所熱衷的龜甲造型上，並不斷加以發揮，使之成為他主要的創作題材。他從平面的甲骨文拓片出發，發展出卜龜浮雕，再由浮雕轉化為立體龜甲造型，並輔以其他古代神話形象，以豐富作品的寓意。甲骨之於張義，此時已不僅僅是一個卜天地、知凶吉的靈物，而是盛載著中國遠古文化及神秘故事的載體（趙錦誠：“尚古的張義藝術”，見《張義雕塑》，香港市政局，1993年）。

1968年，張義在中元畫會第五次會展上展出了木浮雕《原》，這是他以龜甲為造型的最成功的作品之一。該作品由12個形象不同的龜甲浮雕組合而成，外呈方形，方形之內有一個大圓圈。圓圈內的龜甲刻畫較為豐富，上面分布著不規則的蠔宿、殘洞，仿佛是顯微鏡放大下的影像，圓圈外的龜甲造型簡朴，與圈內部分形成鮮明對比，顯示出外方內圓的東方哲學觀點。

《四靈》是另一件有代表性的龜甲題材木雕作品。張義在創作該類作品時，採取透雕手法，將龜甲之間的空隙部分琢去，同時，對於每個龜甲上的裝飾圖案，無論是蠔宿、女陰、虫洞或抽象圖形，也均採用深淺不等和曲直不同的鏤空方式，使作品既流露出質朴的自然意趣，又具有圖騰般的庄穆與深沉。

60年代後期，張義還創作了一批龜形鑄銅小雕塑，這使他的龜甲題材創作顯得更加豐富。

III. “Cast Paper” Period

Having experimented for nearly 10 years with images of bone oracle inscriptions and tortoise shells, and created many large reliefs and fully 3D sculptures of materials like bronze and wood, Cheung Yee proceeded to explore new domains in sculpture from the late 1960s onwards. This time, he developed a deep interest for “cast paper” techniques along with further delving into Chinese elements.

“Cast paper” involves the making of a lead mould by means of a wooden relief, over which self-made paper pulp is pressed, followed by a covering of fibreglass. When air-dried and uncovered, the result is an extraordinary paper relief. Cheung’s inspiration in this genre was aided by his liking for and studies in ancient Chinese papermaking and printing. His cast paper works were of two types – the independent and the compound. The former were made with single templates, whereas the latter required combinations of smaller multiple templates a la ancient movable type printing. The fact that, in the latter case, templates could be disassembled into many smaller independent pieces for various new combinations meant that the artist could cast paper reliefs of different motifs. His red paper relief *Tablet*, for example, was created out of a combination of 126 independent mini-templates in a 6-by-21 arrangement. Within the cartouche of every single mini-template is an abstract motif that has come to be Cheung’s signature design. These include tortoise shells, barnacles, vaginal forms and so on, and not one of them is like any other. The result is a highly interesting overall image that is internally consistent and yet variegated.

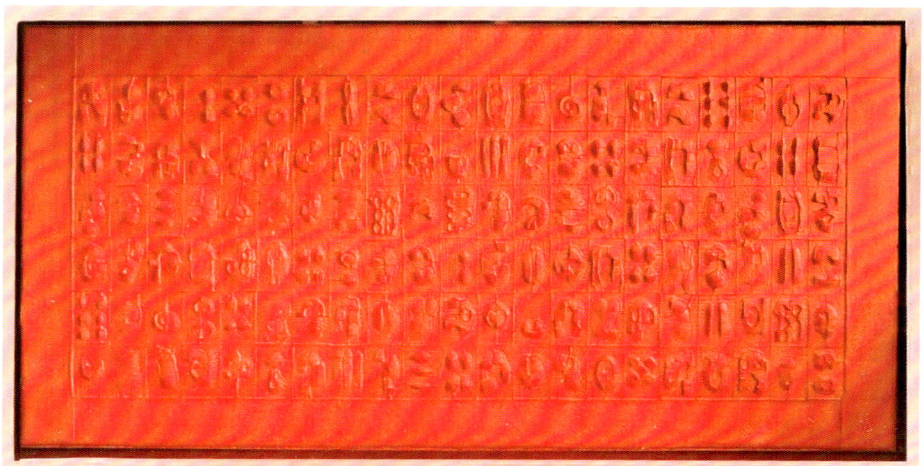

Tablet 銘 , Cast Paper on Wood, 122 x 244 cm, 1976

With the exception of a number of works rendered in pure white, the main colours of Cheung’s paper reliefs are red and black. The former is like ink, whereas the latter is like Chinese vermilion seal paste. This choice of colour was not just about a profound and striking visual impact, but was also made in association with China’s cultural characteristics in high antiquity, which the artist had taken time to study. Ever since the Yellow Thearch initiated the reverence of single colours in 3,000 BC, the dynasties of Xia, Shang, Zhou and Qin had each taken their own chromatic pick. According to the “Great Treatise” in the *Book of Rites*, every change of regime came with a whole new colour for the official court apparel – “The Xia Dynasty was oriented to ink-black, the Shang Dynasty white, and the Zhou Dynasty red”. Black is the colour of the heavens in the *I Ching*, the end of all colours, and the chosen colour of Qin Shi Huang (the first Emperor of China) for garments and banners. Red, on the other hand, was the Zhou

三、“鑄紙”時期

從60年代後期開始，在對甲骨文及龜板造型進行了近10年的探索，採用青銅、木頭等材料創作出許多大型浮雕和圓雕作品後，張義又著手於新的嘗試，對“鑄紙”手法產生了濃厚的興趣，並繼續挖掘中國元素，在雕塑領域開辟出新的天地。

所謂“鑄紙”，是在木板上刻出浮雕，然後用鉛制成模，把自制的紙漿壓在鉛模上，再蓋上玻璃纖維，等風干後揭起，便成為一幅效果奇特的紙浮雕作品。張義的這一種創作靈感，得益於他對中國古代造紙術和印刷術的喜愛和研究。他的紙浮雕作品分為獨立型和複合型兩種，前者由單塊模板制成，後者則如古代活字印刷術，由多塊模板拼合而成。由於後一種模板可拆分成許多獨立的小板塊，並可進行各種新的組合，因而能鑄出各種不同圖形的紙浮雕來。例如，他的紅色紙浮雕《銘》，就是由126塊獨立的模板，按橫6行、豎21列的方式組合而成，每塊模板的橢圓形內，都塑有張義慣用的抽象圖案，如龜甲、蠔宿和女性生殖器官等，沒有一個是重復的。畫面效果既統一又有變化，耐人尋味。

張義的紙浮雕以紅、黑兩色為主（也有一部分採用純白色），黑色似墨，紅如印泥。他選用這兩種顏色，除了追求深沉而強烈的視覺效果外，也與其研究中國上古時期的文化特征有關。公元前三千年，自黃帝開始選擇單色崇拜，夏商周秦各有所好，《禮記》大傳中就記載了各朝代更迭時改用不同顏色的朝服：“夏尚墨、殷尚白，周尚赤”。黑色在《易經》中被認為是天的顏色，是一切顏色的止熄，秦始皇即位後即“易服色與旗色為黑”；紅色作為周朝國色，漢唐以來備受歡迎，象征著吉祥喜慶。張義對於紅黑這兩種深藏著中國哲學與情感的色彩

Dynasty's imperial colour, and a very popular colour since the Han and Tang Dynasty symbolic of auspiciousness and joyous celebration. The colours red and black, thus profoundly charged with Chinese thought and sentiments, were employed by Cheung Yee in such a manner as to instill his works with a deep sense of historicity and mystique. Pure and thick in application, these colours do not appear monotonous on the uneven surfaces of the paper reliefs, but instead shimmer with rich possibilities under different lightings. Cheung Yee's wooden sculptures and paper reliefs from the late 1960s to the 70s demonstrate that he had attained a certain climax in his artistic career. The paper works, in particular, were most representative of his aesthetic pursuit. What were his original intentions when he made these? As Cheung himself had clearly put it, "I hope that when others look at my work, they will mentally associate it with a Chinese artist – one who has Chinese blood in his veins. In fact, I have chosen to work with paper because it is one of the four great inventions of China." (Chen Manyu, "A Baptism of Chinese History and Culture", in *Xingzhou Zhoubao*, December 10, 2000)

During this time, Cheung received some prestigious recognition for his work. In 1978, the Hong Kong Museum of Art put up a solo exhibition in his honour. In the following year, he was awarded a MBE by the Queen of England.

IV. "Crab" Period

Cheung Yee embarked on a new artistic quest from the early 1980s onwards. He was constantly collecting crab specimens and all kinds of artistic figures associated with crabs, hoping to receive some inspiration from them. While the crab and the tortoise are both crawling shelled creatures alike in colour and form, the latter tends to be static and reserved, whereas the former is active and outspreading. The two also differ in terms of mien and spatiality. Cheung's shift of creative focus from the tortoise to the crab was very much in line with his creative trajectory and aesthetic orientation. It also provided a foothold for him to actualise sculptural innovation.

Cheung Yee displayed his cast bronze crab *Crab #1* for the first time when the Hong Kong Urban Council and the Hong Kong Sculptors Association held the Modern Outdoor Sculpture Exhibition in 1984. Precast bronze segments were made via moulding and then connected together with stainless steel screws to form this giant crustacean 4.5 metres in height. All eight legs touch the ground, while the two pincers are positioned on the crab's shell in the shape of a T. The entire structure is like a pavilion. The process of making it is nothing less than a demonstration of the artist's lofty spirit and incredible creativity. Between 1984 and 1985,

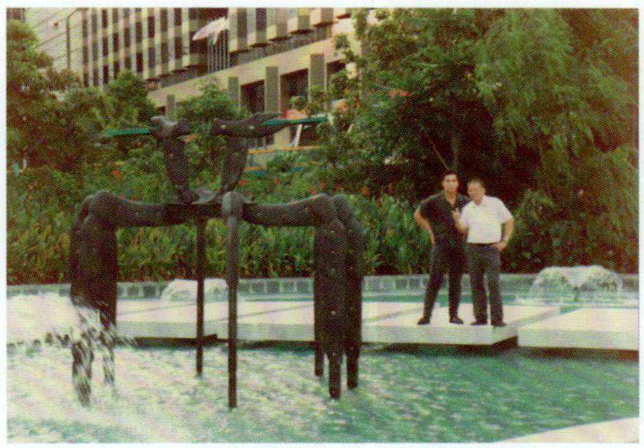

Crab #1 將軍一號 , Bronze, 450 cm high, 1984

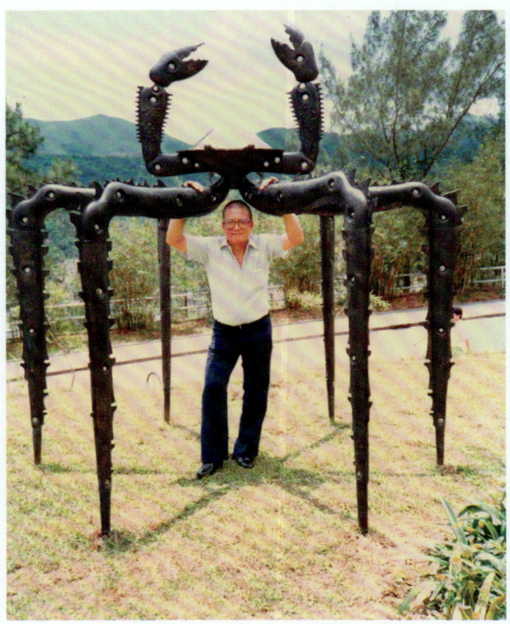

Crab #2 將軍#二 , Bronze, 300 cm high, 1984

的運用，使其作品具有極為深厚的歷史感和神秘感。這些單純而濃厚的紅色或黑色，在凹凸不平的紙浮雕上不僅不顯得單調，反而隨著光源的不同而產生豐富的變化。

張義於60年代後期和70年代所作的木雕和紙浮雕，顯示出他在藝術上已進入到一個高峰期，其中紙浮雕最能體現他的美學追求。對於這方面創作初衷，他曾作過明確的表達："我希望別人看我的作品時，會聯想到它出自一個華人之手，流著炎黃子孫的血液。選擇以紙創作，也是因為它是中國四大發明之一。"（陳曼玉："中國歷史文化的洗禮"，見《星州周報》，2000年12月10日）

1978年，香港藝術館為他舉辦了個人展覽。翌年，英國女皇又頒授MBE勛銜給他，這些都是對他藝術成就的肯定。

四、"螃蟹"時期

從80年代初起，張義開始新的藝術征程。他不斷收集螃蟹標本或以螃蟹為題的各種藝術造型，希望從中得到一些啟示。螃蟹與龜均為甲殼類爬行動物，在色澤與造型上頗為相似，但龜態靜而蟹勢動，龜內斂而蟹張揚，兩者的神態和空間感又各不相同。張義把創作題材從龜轉到蟹，既順應了他的創作思路與美學取向，又為他的雕塑創新提供了依托。

1984年，在香港市政局及香港雕塑家協會舉辦的"現代戶外雕塑展"上，張義首次展出了他的鑄銅螃蟹《將軍一號》。這件大型銅蟹是利用翻沙模子鑄銅技術分段鑄成，再以不鏽鋼螺絲加以連接。銅蟹身高4.5米，八足著地，雙鉗成丁字形置於蟹殼上，整個結構如同一座亭子，其創作過程顯示了藝術家的氣概與創造力。從1984年到1985年間，張義採用分段澆鑄方式共創作了四件螃蟹雕塑，每一件都有不同的特

Cheung created a total of four crab sculptures by means of segmental precasting, each special in its own way. Other than the abovementioned *Crab #1*, there is the second piece known as *Crab #2*, which is similar to *#1* in size but has two legs less. In this piece, the influence of the Shang Dynasty bronze vessels known as *zun* is unmistakable as prominent spines line the inner and outer edges of every leg with robust decorativeness. The third crab is relatively smaller, though still slightly taller than an average person. Not only does it stand upright on long straightened legs, it also comes with four round breasts. The fourth crab, known as *Crab #4*, is the smallest of them all. Here, the crab's shell, legs and pincers have been freely recombined in a fashion that is far removed from the creature's natural configuration but fully demonstrative of the domineering mannerism of crabs.

The evolution of Cheung Yee's crab sculptures from semi-abstraction to full-fledged abstraction is similar to that of his tortoise shell works. It reflects Cheung's powers of artistic generalisation, as well as his courage to pursue novelty aggressively and to constantly challenge himself. Speaking about the crab sculptures, he once said, "In my mind, the crab might not be just a crab. It could be a person, a god, a building, or even an abstract construct" (Zhao Jincheng, "Cheung Yee's Archetropic Art", in *Cheung Yee's Sculptures* (Hong Kong: Hong Kong Urban Council, 1993))- thus is his ardent quest in art for a unity of Nature and Man, and of object and subject.

V. Period of Integrative Evolution

From the late 1980s on till this day, Cheung Yee has, in continuation of his existing line of creative thought, introduced other elements from China's distant past into his own wooden sculptures – the *Hetu* (Yellow River Diagram), *Luoshu* (Luo River Writing), Four Signs and Eight Trigrams. His artistic sentiments are harking back to a further source of ethnic culture.

The *Hetu* and *Luoshu* represent the earliest Chinese's understanding and generalisation of Nature. They have always been regarded as the very beginning of Chinese civilisation around the Yellow River basin, and have been hailed "cosmic magic squares". Like the Eight Trigrams reputedly derived from the *Hetu* by the mythological figure Fu Xi, these diagrams are the sources of the *Zhou Yi* (i.e., the *I Ching* and its expositions), highly concise but containing endless possibilities. Cheung Yee has managed to assimilate these foundational symbols of the Chinese civilisation into his art, thereby instilling his works with a numinous touch and a certain pensiveness, such that they embody his vision and explorations of Nature's unfathomable secrets.

Notably, Cheung Yee's paper reliefs have also undergone certain changes since the 1990s. One sees greater flexibility and freedom in the choice of patterns. The colours too have gone beyond the original symbolism to venture into freer and livelier pointillism. Dots of many different colours such as white, purple, pink and orange come together

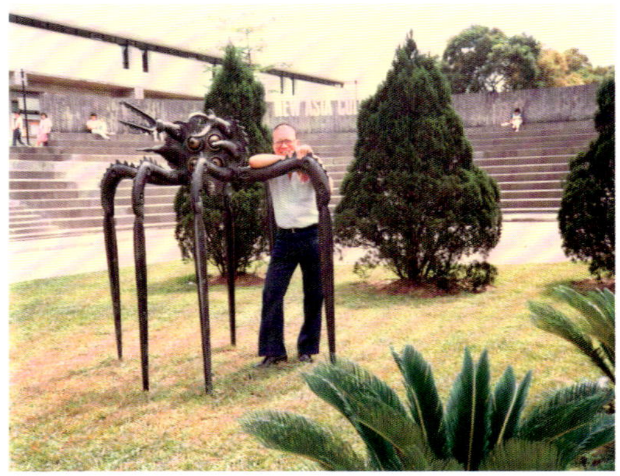

Crab #3 螃蟹#三 , Bronze, 200 cm high, 1984

點。除了上述《將軍一號》，第二件取名《將軍#二》，大小與一號相近，只是少了兩條腿，而每條腿的內外緣均有突出的稜脊，明顯受到商代青銅器“尊”的影響，有較強的裝飾性；第三件螃蟹形體較小，僅略高於常人，造型乃取長腿直立的方式，身體部分也直立，並且有四個圓渾的乳房；第四件螃蟹取名《跋扈將軍#四》，體積最小，蟹殼、蟹腿和蟹鉗完全脫離自然形態，在自由組合下充分表現出螃蟹的跋扈橫行之勢。

張義的螃蟹雕塑從半抽象到抽象，演變過程一如龜甲雕塑，這反映出他的藝術概括力和銳意創新、不斷挑戰自我的勇氣。他在談及螃蟹造型時說：“其實蟹在我心目中不一定是蟹，可能是一個人，或是一個神，又或是一座建築物，甚至是一件抽象架構。”（趙錦誠：“尚古的張義藝術”，見《張義雕塑》，香港市政局，1993年）可見他這類在創作中，力求達到天人合一、物我兩忘的境地。

五、綜合衍化時期

從80年代末至今，張義在延續既有的創作思路的同時，還把中國上古時期的河圖洛書與四象八卦引入到自己的木雕作品中，藝術情思上溯到更為遙遠的民族文化根源。

河圖洛書乃華夏始祖對大自然的體悟和歸納，歷來被認為是河洛文化的濫觴、中華文明的源頭，有“宇宙魔方”之譽。河圖與洛書，以及傳說中伏羲依據河圖畫出的八卦，圖形都極簡練，但變幻無窮，為周易來源。張義將這些中華文明的基本符號吸收到藝術創作中，從而使自己的作品充滿了靈性與幽思，體現出對深邃莫測的自然奧秘的憧憬和探究。

90年代以來，張義的紙浮雕也出現了一些變化，圖案的選擇更加靈活自由，色彩上也打破原有的象征性，開始嘗試自由活潑的點彩方式，即將白色、紫色、桃紅、橘黃等多種顏色點染於同一作品上，使紙浮雕不僅具有先前那種令人震懾的庄穆感，而且還有令人輕鬆愉快的一面。

in a single artwork, such that the paper reliefs take on some lightheartedness without losing the awe-inspiring solemnity of the earlier works.

In half a century of sculpting, Cheung Yee's style has changed in accordance with different materials or themes, yet a common thread runs through his oeuvre – his passion for traditional Chinese culture, as well as his tenacious pursuit for modern art of a style that is truly Hong Kong's (and indeed Chinese). Throughout the development of his art, Cheung Yee has adhered closely to both variations and canonicity. He has always maintained intriguing dichotomies - Western framework / Eastern philosophy, and modern language / very ancient enigmas - in an indivisible whole, as if the barriers of time and space have been dissipated in the artist's all-apprehending psyche.

張義在長達半個世紀的雕塑創作中，風格或因材料變化而變化，或因題材不同而不同，但貫穿始終的，是他對中華傳統文化的熱愛和對香港乃至中國風格現代藝術的執著追求。縱觀他的創作歷程，“易”與“經”如影隨形，西方架構與東方哲學、現代語言與遠古幽秘始終渾然一體。時間與空間的阻隔，彷彿已消融於藝術家通悟的心靈。

About Dr Zhu Qi:

Born in Wenzhou, Zhejiang, Dr Zhu Qi has played a pivotal role in the Chinese cultural exchange. Presently, he is Cultural Counselor at the Embassy of the People's Republic of China in the Republic of Singapore. Having obtained a doctorate from the Central Academy of Fine Arts, he is also an established writer, having written several books on fine arts. These include Solidification of Feeling: Sculpture; History of Hong Kong Art; Random Talk about Buddhist Art; and Ju Ming. His published essays are: A Brief Study of Feng Zikai's Viewpoint of Art and the Feature of His Mantra; and Øverview of Hong Kong Visual Arts; Modern Chinese Sculptures.

朱琦博士簡介

1964年生於浙江台州。長期從事中外文化交流工作，現為中國駐新加坡大使館文化參贊。中國美術學院美術學博士。出版專著有《詩情凝固：雕塑》、《香港美術史》、《佛教美術漫談》、《朱銘》。發表論文包括《曲高和眾，雅俗共賞：試論豐子愷的藝術觀及其漫畫特征》、《香港美術概論》、《現代語境中的中國雕塑》等等。

An Interview with Cheung Yee

張義訪談錄

In the following interview, Zhu Qi is the questioner, with replies given by Cheung Yee.

ZHU: When you were studying in Hong Kong's Tak Ming Middle School, you once came under the tutelage of Ting Yen Yung. Later on, you studied traditional Chinese realistic painting and seal carving in the Art Department of the Taiwan Normal University. What made you switch to sculpting?

CHEUNG: I studied in a teachers training college. I was supposed to teach art after graduating. So, I had to get involved with all kinds of art and not study one discipline alone. Nevertheless, when it came to courses I liked, I was driven by interest to study a little more. For instance, I liked the seal carving classes taught by Wang Zhuang, so I was willing to spend more time on that, and hence received greater inspiration from that too. I have a liking for all sorts of craftwork ever since my childhood. It is pleasurable to feel and touch something with one's hands. Eventually, when I discovered that the works of Oriental or Chinese sculptors were rarely seen in major international art exhibitions, a desire arose in me to sculpt 3D figures and bring pride to the Chinese people.

ZHU: I feel that the traditional art training you received in the early days has influenced your sculpture in at least two aspects. In terms of aesthetic taste, it makes you inclined towards numinousness, philosophical depth and mystique. In terms of artistic vocabulary, it moves you to unconsciously pursue the allure of symbolisms, randomness and traditional lines. What do you think?

CHEUNG: That is indeed so. Major sources of influence on my sculptures include various kinds of ancient Chinese carvings and calligraphy. In the area of calligraphy, my favourites are the works of Huai Su, Xu Wei, Bada Shanren, Jin Nong, Zheng Xie (Zheng Banqiao), Xu Shengweng, Deng Erya and so on.

ZHU: Which of the ancient Chinese carvings have the most profound influence on you?

CHEUNG: That, first and foremost, would be the bronzes – especially bronzes of the Shang Dynasty, Eastern Zhou and Western Zhou period in the form of animals. The next in line would be the wooden sculptures and lacquerware of the state of Chu, followed by Han Dynasty wooden and pottery figurines, the large cliff grottoes of the Wei, Jin, Northern and Southern Dynasties, and so on. I have also collected many painted tiles and rubbings of cliff figures.

ZHU: The British sculptor Henry Moore had apparently influenced your early sculptures too. In what way did Moore's work inspire you?

CHEUNG: Henry Moore's totem-like sculptures had indeed moved me profoundly with their extremely primitive yet modern look. I first saw his works in foreign magazines. The one that left me the deepest impression was the sculpture of a gigantic feminine body. It was magnificent, like a mountain or a cave. It reminded one of Nature. I used to be deeply influenced by such works, but I gave up on them soon. I felt that I should go my own way.

以下訪談為朱琦問，張義答

朱：你在香港德明中學讀書時，曾受教於丁衍庸，後又在台灣師范大學藝術系學習中國傳統工筆畫和篆刻，是什麼原因使你改而從事雕塑創作的？

張：我讀的是師范大學，畢業後要從事美術教育，因此，在校時對各個藝術門類均要有所涉及，不能專修某一項。不過，自己喜好什麼課程，就憑興致多學一點。比如，我喜歡王壯為老師的篆刻課，願意化較多的時間去學，從中得到的啟發也就大一些。我自幼喜歡各類手工勞作，手的觸覺使人產生喜悅和快感。後來發現國際藝術大展中很少有東方或華人雕塑家的作品，因而萌發了從事立體制作，為中國人爭光的願望。

朱：我覺得你早期所接受的傳統藝術教育，至少在兩個方面影響了你的雕塑創作：一是在審美情趣上，使你偏愛靈性、哲理和神秘感；二是在藝術語言上，使你不自覺地追求象征性、隨機性和傳統線條的韻味。你自己對於這一點是如何看的？

張：的確如此。對我雕塑創作產生過重要影響的包括各類中國古代雕刻和書法。在書法方面，我比較喜歡懷素、徐青藤、八大山人、金農、鄭板橋、徐生翁、鄧爾雅等人的作品。

朱：對你影響最深的中國古代雕刻是什麼？

張：首先是青銅器，尤其是殷商和西周、東周時期的各種青銅動物造型；其次是楚木雕、漆器，漢木俑、陶俑，魏晉南北朝的各類大型摩崖石窟等。我還收集了許多畫像磚、摩崖造像拓本。

朱：從你早期的雕塑來看，似乎還受到英國雕塑家亨利•摩爾的影響。摩爾的雕塑給過你什麼啟示？

張：亨利•摩爾的圖騰般的雕塑既非常原始，又具有濃厚的現代氣息，的確曾深深地打動我。我最初是從外國雜志上看到他的作品的，印象最深的是巨型女體雕塑，形象如山如窟，蔚為大觀，使人聯想到了大自然。我最初曾深受這類作品影響，但後來很快又放棄了，覺得還是應走自己的路。

ZHU: As I recall, Hong Kong artists such as yourself and Ku Mei have talked about personally received influence from Zao Wou Ki during the 1950s and 60s. Is such influence embodied in the way you perceive and deal with the relationship between the traditional Chinese spirit and modern Western art? What is your assessment of Zao Wou Ki's art and influence?

CHEUNG: I knew about Paris' Zao Wou Ki when I was a student. I saw some of his early works. Not only do they incorporate elements of Chinese calligraphy ranging from oracle bone inscriptions, ancient bronze inscriptions to cursive scripts, they also embody sentiments of Chinese landscape paintings. They are truly remarkable. At that time, I admired him greatly for showing the international art circles what Chinese art (and indeed Oriental art in general) could do. We may say that Zao Wou Ki had influenced a whole generation of young Chinese artists outside of the mainland. All of our art had more or less been influenced by him.

ZHU: Your early works reveal a special liking for the tortoise shell theme. Did this stem from your interest in the art of calligraphy?

CHEUNG: The inspiration for the shells came by chance when I was studying rubbings of oracle bone inscriptions. All of a sudden, I saw that the rubbings themselves are excellent forms. So, I applied them to printmaking and relief sculpting.

ZHU: Structurally speaking, are your large combinatory wooden carvings influenced by ancient movable type printing? What is the meaning of the tortoise shells, barnacles, vaginal forms and other abstract patterns that you employ so frequently?

CHEUNG: In terms of structure and manner of production, my large wooden reliefs and paper reliefs (also known as cast paper prints) are indeed influenced by ancient rubbings and movable type printing. The abstract symbols in these works - including female genitalia, barnacles, shells, tortoise shell pieces, cracks and gaping holes - express Chinese philosophical notions such as *Yin* / *Yang*, Heaven / Earth, square / circle, positivity / negativity, movement / stillness and so on. I like the *I Ching*, but I have not delved deep into it. What I have grasped are merely the absolute basics, the most fundamental ideas, such as the genesis of existence from non-existence. In this genesis, there is chaos in the beginning; one is divided into two, and then into four, and subsequently eight. Another example would be the dichotomies in Nature, such as Heaven and Earth, and *Yin* and *Yang*, which constitute the *Dao*. The "*I*" of the *I Ching* refers to changes. Only with changes can there be vitality and innovation. In my artistic practice, I like to use curves and circles. Where there is a circle in a square, you get movement in the midst of stillness, which yields an appearance of greater simplicity and vigour. I also like water. It can either be formless or take a particular form. It takes the shape of whatever container it is held in. What I mean by "water" also includes alcohol, which has a fiery quality

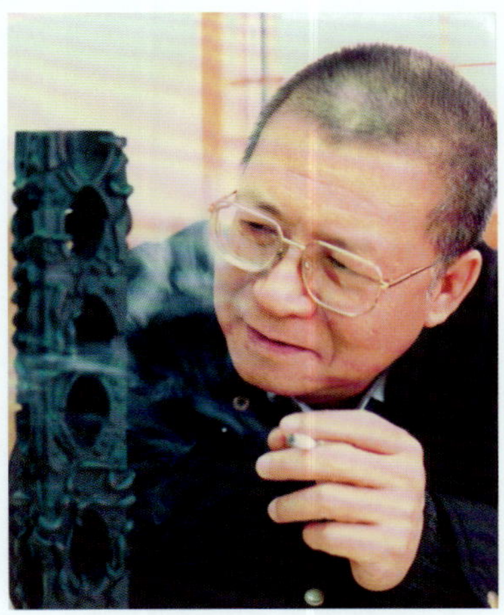

Cheung Yee with his work, Totem 圖騰

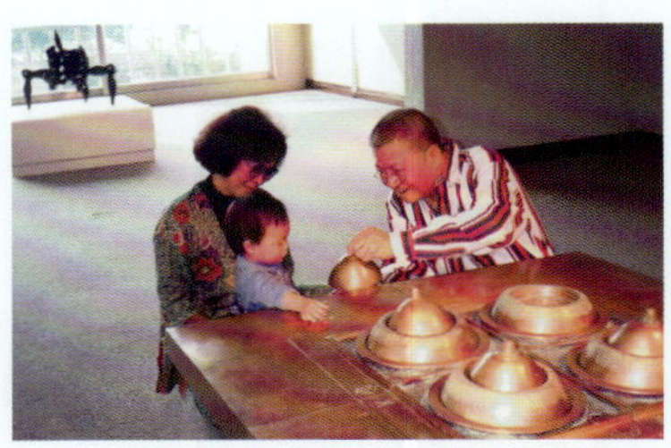

Cheung Yee, his wife and grandchild, The Tablet 大地四方

朱：記得你和顧媚等香港藝術家都曾談起過趙無極在上世紀50、60年代給予你們的影響，這是否體現在對中國傳統精神與西方現代藝術的關系的認識和處理上？你對趙無極的藝術及其影響力是如何評價的？

張：我在做學生時，就知道巴黎有個趙無極，也看到過他的一些早期作品，這些作品吸收了甲骨文、金文、草書等中國書法元素，包含了中國山水畫的情懷，真是棒極了。我那時對他在國際藝壇上弘揚中國乃至東方藝術感到十分敬佩。可以說，趙無極影響了整整一代大陸以外的中國青年藝術家，我們的藝術或多或少都受到過他的影響。

朱：在早期的創作中，你對龜甲題材情有獨鐘，這是否源於你對於書法藝術的興趣？

張：我確實是在研讀甲骨文拓片時，意外地獲得這一創作靈感的。我當時突然覺得，這拓片本身就是一種很好的造型，於是就把它運用到版畫和浮雕上。

朱：你的大型組合木雕作品，在結構上是否受古代活字印刷術的影響？將龜甲、蠔宿和女性生殖器官等作為慣用的抽象圖案，寓意如何？

張：我的大型木浮雕和紙浮雕（或稱鑄紙版畫），在結構和創作方式上受到古代拓片和活字印刷術的影響。作品中的一些抽象符號，包括女陰、蠔宿、甲殼、龜片、裂縫、空洞等等，寓含著陰陽、天地、方圓、正負、動靜等中國哲學理念。我喜愛《易經》，但研究不深，所了解的只是最基礎的東西，但也是最基本的道理。比如無中生有，開始是混沌，一分為二，再分為四，再分為八。又如大自然中的天地、陰陽等對立存在，即“道”。“易”，也就是“變動”。只有“變動”才有生機，才有創新。我在創作時喜歡用曲線、圓形，方中有圓、靜裡有動，這樣顯得更渾厚些。我也喜歡水，可以無形也可以有形，裝在什麼樣的容器中就呈什麼樣的形。這水也可以是酒，內藏火的個性。

inherent to it.

ZHU: When did you begin working on paper reliefs? How did the inspiration for them come about?

CHEUNG: My work on paper reliefs began in the late 1960s. The inspiration for them came by chance. Now, I have always been an enthusiast of papermaking techniques of the ancient Chinese and minority ethnic groups. I was eating almond cookies one day when I was struck by the form of the cookie. It occurred to me that I could produce very interesting bas-reliefs if I use reliefs to make moulds and then cast works out of self-made paper pulp. Before long, I found myself attempting to do just that. I make both wooden and earthen templates. Some are entirely self-made, or a result of some processing of ready-made objects. The paper employed also varied – sometimes I use a mixture, sometimes a single ingredient. Some of the arranged patterns look like printed texts, and some, inscriptions on bronzes. In the making of paper reliefs, my favourite colour is the Chinese variety of bright red. It is very primitive and rich. I also like to use black, because it, being the father of all colours, can in a sense "lead" the other colours. It signifies the cosmic genesis, an imminent stabilisation of the world.

ZHU: The paper reliefs are rich in Oriental flavour and Chinese cultural significance in every aspect, from the choice of material, method of production, down to the motif designs and the use of specific colours. Was this your original intention?

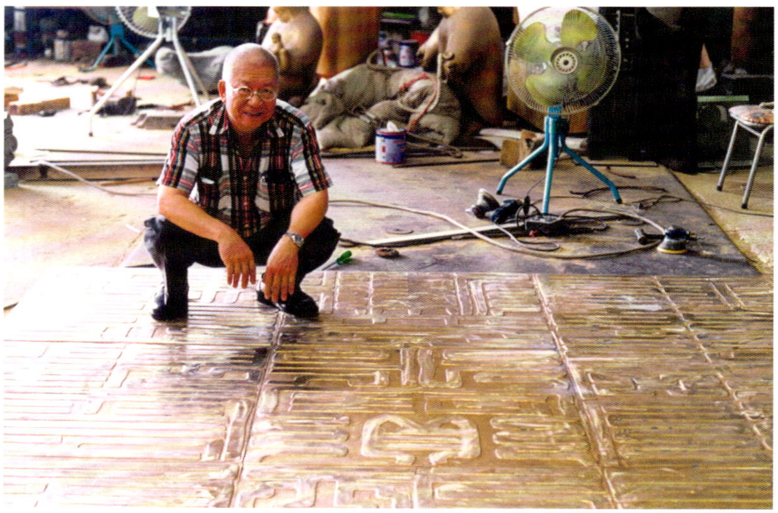

Cheung Yee and his work ~ Seal 印信, Taipei 101, Taiwan

CHEUNG: I wouldn't say I intended things to be so right from the beginning. Rather, these were rediscoveries I made after prolonged and cumulative explorations. After graduating from university, I was exposed to various cultures. I engaged in all kinds of experimentations, including – as mentioned just now – imitations of Henry Moore's works. Yet traditional Chinese culture remains my utmost favourite. It is pretty much an inexhaustible source of inspiration. In art, I wish to go my own way. An artwork must possess one's own style and ethnic spirit.

ZHU: Your paper reliefs have a unique place in sculpture. What is your own view on that?

CHEUNG: My paper reliefs are relatively special. They may inspire later artists in some way, but I wouldn't say they make any special contribution to the fields of sculpture and printmaking.

ZHU: Is the emergence of the cast bronze crabs a mark of your interest in public sculptures?

CHEUNG: I wouldn't say I have such interests. I merely wished to

朱：紙浮雕創作始於何時？創作靈感又是如何產生的？

張：我的紙浮雕創作開始於1960年代後期，創作靈感也得之偶然。我一向喜歡中國古代和各少數民族的造紙技術，有一天吃杏仁餅，從餅的造型中，我聯想到如果用浮雕制模，再用自制的紙漿來鑄，所產生的淺浮雕效果一定很有意思。不久我就開始這樣的嘗試。我制作的模版有木雕，也有泥塑，有自制的，也有選用現成品加工而成的。紙料也多種多樣，有混料，有單料。圖紋的排列，有像印刷字體，又有像青銅器的銘文。我在創作紙浮雕作品時，最喜歡用的是中國的大紅，非常原始、渾厚，同時也喜歡用黑色，因為黑乃眾色之父，能統領眾色，含有混沌初開、乾坤將定之義。

朱：紙浮雕從材料選擇到制作方式、圖案造型乃至色彩運用，處處流露出濃厚的東方特色和中國文化內涵，這些是否皆出於你的初衷？

張：不敢說是初衷，而是不斷積累，在經過一段時期的探索後重新發現的。大學畢業後，我曾接觸過不同文化，進行過多種嘗試，包括上面談到模仿過亨利•摩爾的作品，不過最喜歡的還是中國的傳統文化，這可以說是取之不竭的靈感源泉。我在藝術上希望走的是自己的路，作品一定要有自己的風格和民族氣息。

朱：紙浮雕的創作對整個雕塑界具有獨特的意義，你本人是如何看待的？

張：我的紙浮雕較有特色，可能給後來者一個啟發，但不敢說對雕塑界、版畫界有什麼特殊的貢獻。

朱：鑄銅螃蟹的出現，是否標志著你對公共雕塑的興趣？

張：談不上有這方面的興趣，只是想自然地去創作、自由地去表現。鑄銅螃蟹最初的體積還較小，後來越做越大，比人還高，因此只能放到室外，讓觀者可以觸摸、穿越，小孩子可

create art naturally, and express myself freely. The cast bronze crabs were initially smaller in size, but they got bigger as the work went on, even taller than a man. For this reason, they can only be erected outdoors, where viewers can touch and pass through them, and where children can climb and play with them. Sculptures like these become closer to people, and the two mingle as one. This seems to endow the works with some kind of timelessness.

ZHU: As I recall, you once said that in your mind, the crab might not be just a crab – that it could be a person, a god, a building, or an abstract construct. Now, the choice of the crab as a sculptural subject is obviously a continuation from the tortoise shell to some extent. Yet, was room for greater creative possibilities part of your consideration too?

CHEUNG: Yes. The crab is a metaphor for a man or a god. Due to its distinct structuredness, a crab is like a living piece of miniature architecture. It is like a pavilion or a shed, complete with shadows and space. It can look very different in winter, in summer, in rain or in snow. There are indeed similarities between crabs and tortoise shells. I started out with the latter as a subject matter, but moved on to crabs mainly because I became intrigued by the crustacean's structure. Both the tortoise and the crab are commonly featured in traditional art in the first place. Originally, I could have made the cast bronze crabs even larger, but I was limited by private space and finances. For now, they can only be the way they are, due to my lack of means. If I have an opportunity in the future, I can try again.

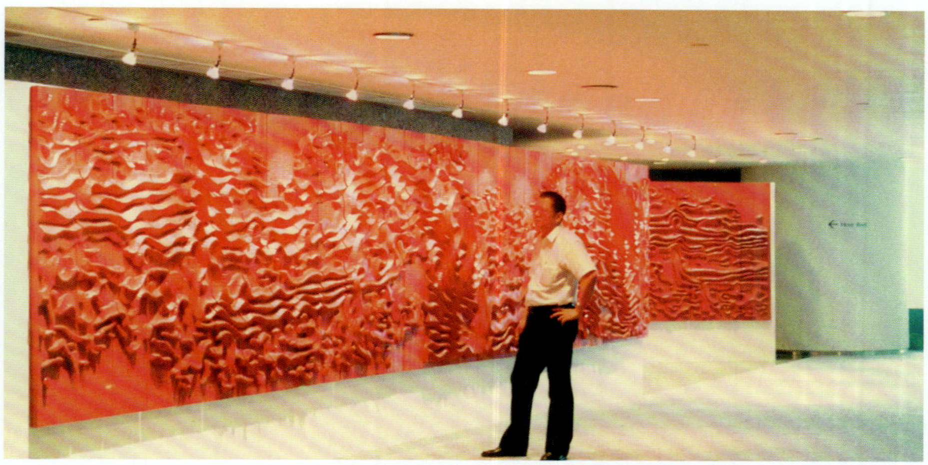

Cheung Yee and his work, The Earth 山河大地, *Convention Centre, Hong Kong*

ZHU: In sculpting the crabs, you carried out a series of experimentations and had managed not to cover the same ground twice. In retrospect, which crab is it that best embodies your artistic intent and your idea of the crab-god?

CHEUNG: The best articulation of my understanding of the form of the crab would be *Crab #4*.

ZHU: In the early years, you participated actively in the Chung Yuen Art Society's activities. The Society was arguably the mainstay of Hong Kong's modern art. It connected with the legacy of the Hong Kong Artists Association, and led to the formation of groups like the Hong Kong Visual Artists Society. The Society had an outstanding place in the history of Hong Kong's modern art from the 60s to the 70s. How do you view this part of history and the role you played in it?

CHEUNG: I was a founding member of the Chung Yuen Art Society,

以攀爬、游戲。這樣，雕塑和人的接觸距離拉近，合而為一，這樣作品似乎也有了一些永恆性。

朱：記得你曾說過：螃蟹在你心目中不一定是蟹，可能是一個人、一個神，或是一座建築物、一件抽象架構。選擇螃蟹作為造型對象，與龜甲顯然有一定的延續性，不過，是否還考慮到有更大的造型空間？

張：是的，螃蟹隱喻人或神。由於蟹的架構性強，所以像一座活的小建築，一座亭子或一個棚架，有空間、有投影，有冬夏雨雪之不同，很有變化。螃蟹與龜甲確有相似性，我先以龜甲為題材，後又延伸到螃蟹，主要是因為它們的結構所吸引，而這兩者也是傳統藝術中的常見題材。鑄銅螃蟹本來還可以做得更大，但因我的私人空間和財力有限，缺少創作條件，目前只能如此，將來如有機會，可以一試。

朱：在螃蟹的塑造中，你進行了一系列探索，從不重復。現在回頭來看，最能體現你造型意圖以及螃蟹之神的應屬哪一件？

張：最能道出我對螃蟹造型的理解是“跋扈將軍”這一件。

朱：你早年在香港積極參與“中元畫會”的活動，該畫會堪稱是香港現代藝術的中堅，它上承“香港藝術家協會”，下啟“香港視覺藝術家協會”，在整個60至70年代香港現代藝術發展中具有突出的地位。你對這樣一段歷史以及自己所起的作用有何評價？

張：我是“中元畫會”的創會會員，也是最早從事雕塑創作的成員。其他成員如林鎮輝當時也曾用焊接技術創作過立體作品，文樓從事雕塑創作的時間稍晚些。搞雕塑其實是很孤獨的，許多人為了某種原因不敢從事，或者半途而廢。這種工作需要一股“笨”勁，不能像他人可以躲在冷氣房裡。

and the first of its members to engage in sculpting. Other members – such as Lin Zhenhui – had produced 3D works by means of welding in those days. Van Lau started sculpting somewhat later. Sculpting is actually a very lonely business. Many people shrink from it for certain reasons, or give up along the way. One needs to be driven with almost moronic commitment to do this work. One cannot stay all day in an air-conditioned room like everybody else.

ZHU: We have not seen you produce new works for the last few years. Could you talk about the current status of your work? What is your mentality now?

CHEUNG: Although I have retired from teaching, I'm still very busy now, mainly engaged in studying scripts and calligraphy, enhancing papermaking, and sculpting wood. My hands can't stay idle. Only by staying constantly busy can I feel happy and close to Nature.

ZHU: In your artistic career of almost half a century, you have never ceased to explore and experiment. Would this be a reflection of your own perspective on art?

CHEUNG: I'm always busy every day, constantly feeling, exploring and discovering. I hope I can produce more works someday for viewers. I used to be impatient, constantly racing against time. Now I run on a slower beat. I'm more at ease, but still not daring to become sluggish. My perspective on art is very simple: one has to draw from a wide range of sources. Your inspiration may come from tradition, or you can pick up new ideas and challenges from art of the newer generations. The cosmic "*I*" is always changing. To change is to be timeless.

朱：最近幾年沒有看到你的新作，能否談談你的創作現狀和體會？

張：我在教學上雖然已經退休，但還是很忙碌的，主要忙於研究字體、書法，改進造紙術，也刻些木雕，一雙手總是停不下來。只有這樣，我才感到快樂，才能接近自然。

朱：從事藝術創作近半個世紀，你從未停止過探索，這是不是反映出你的藝術觀？

張：我每天都忙不停，不斷地感受、探索、發現，希望他日能有更多的作品奉獻給觀眾。以前，我總是很著急，與時間賽跑，現在節奏放慢了，悠然自在些，但也不敢懈怠。我的藝術觀很簡單，就是廣採博納，可以從傳統中得到靈感，也可從新生代藝術中得到啟發和挑戰。"易"者常變，變幻才是永恆。

Sculpture
雕塑

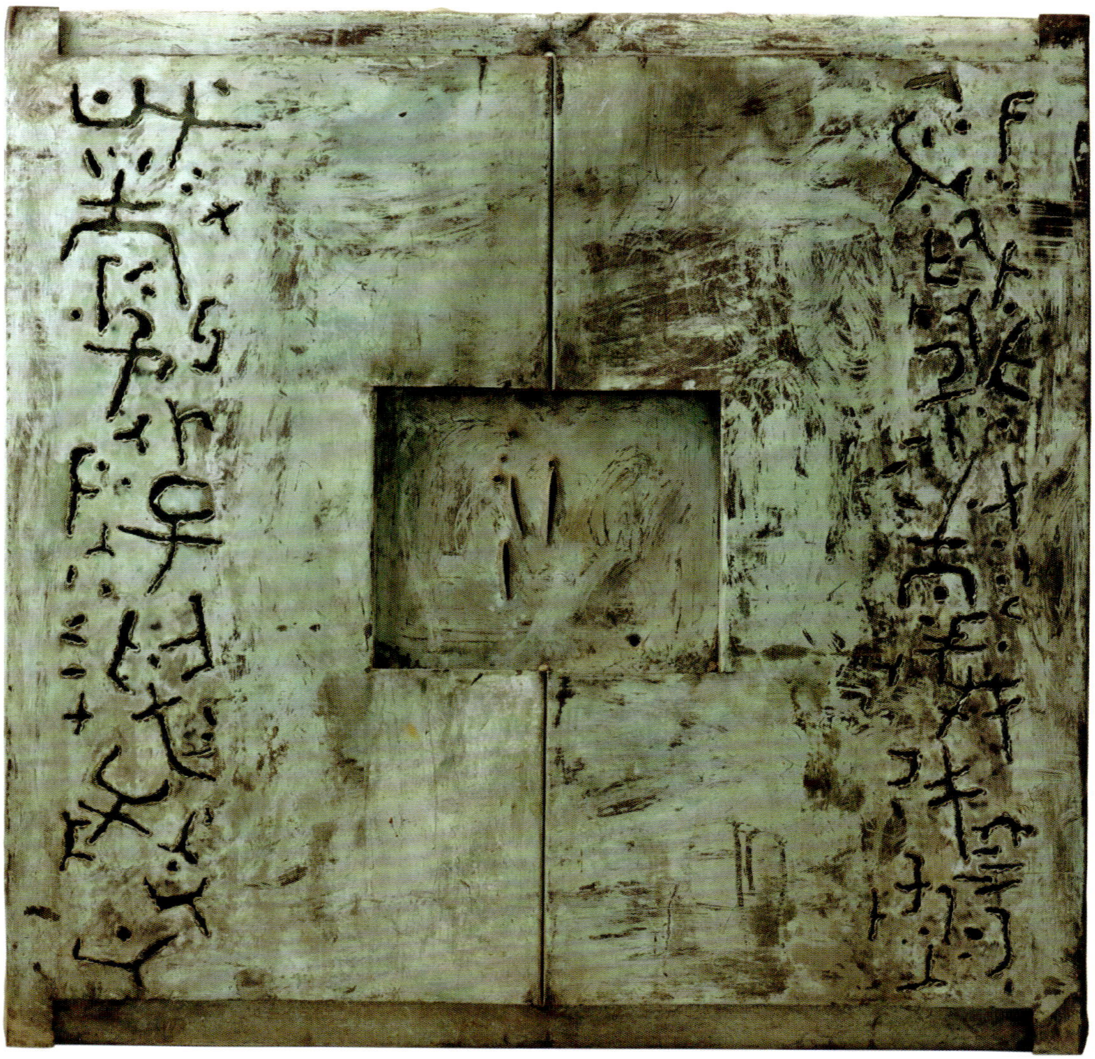

DOOR
門
Bronze
112 x 112 cm
1964

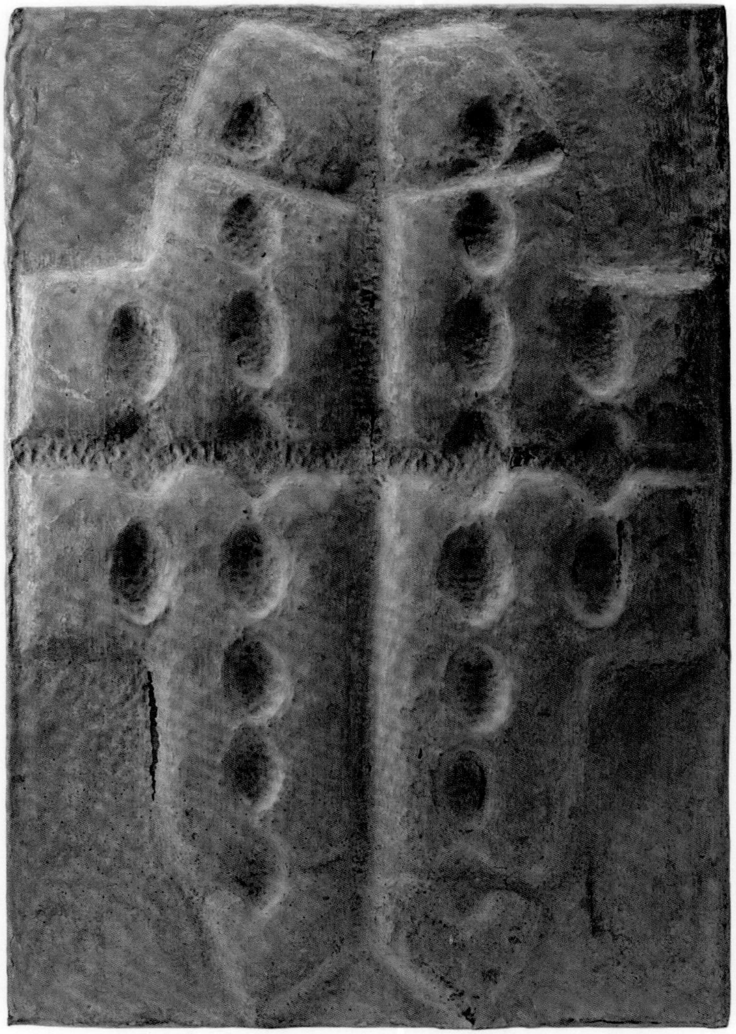

FORTUNE
福
Bronze
113 x 77 cm
1964

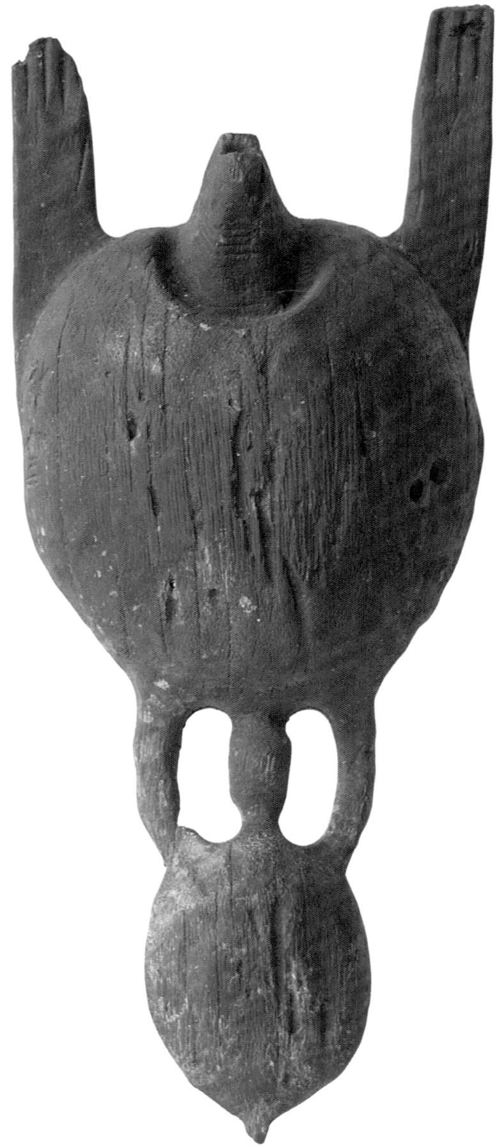

MOTHER & CHILD
母子
Bronze
34 x 15 cm
1964

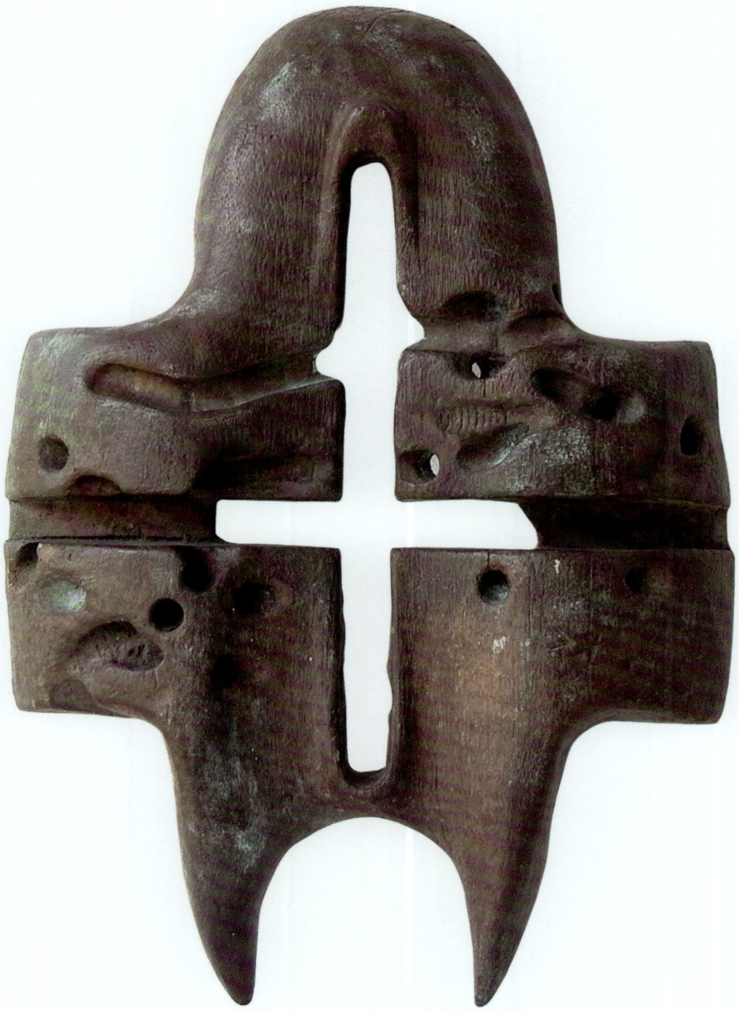

FORTUNE
卜
Bronze
31 x 22 cm
1968

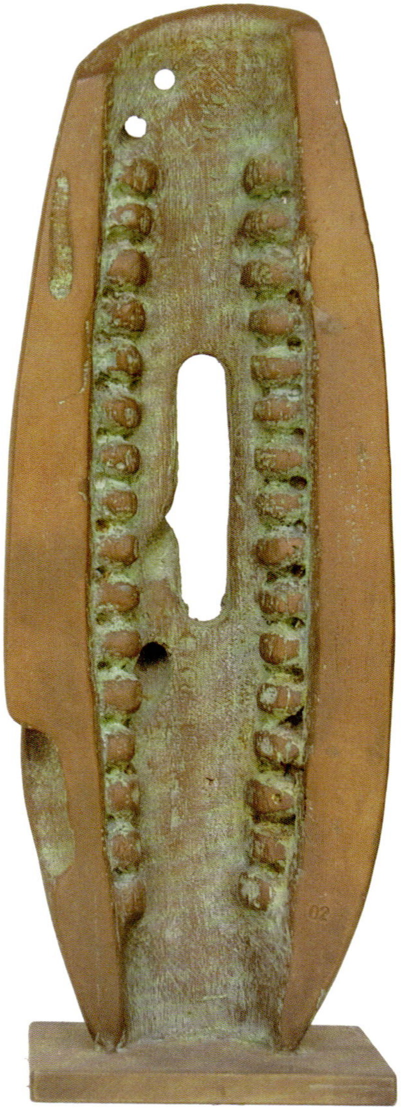

FEMALE
坤儀
Bronze
30 x 10 x 9 cm
1968

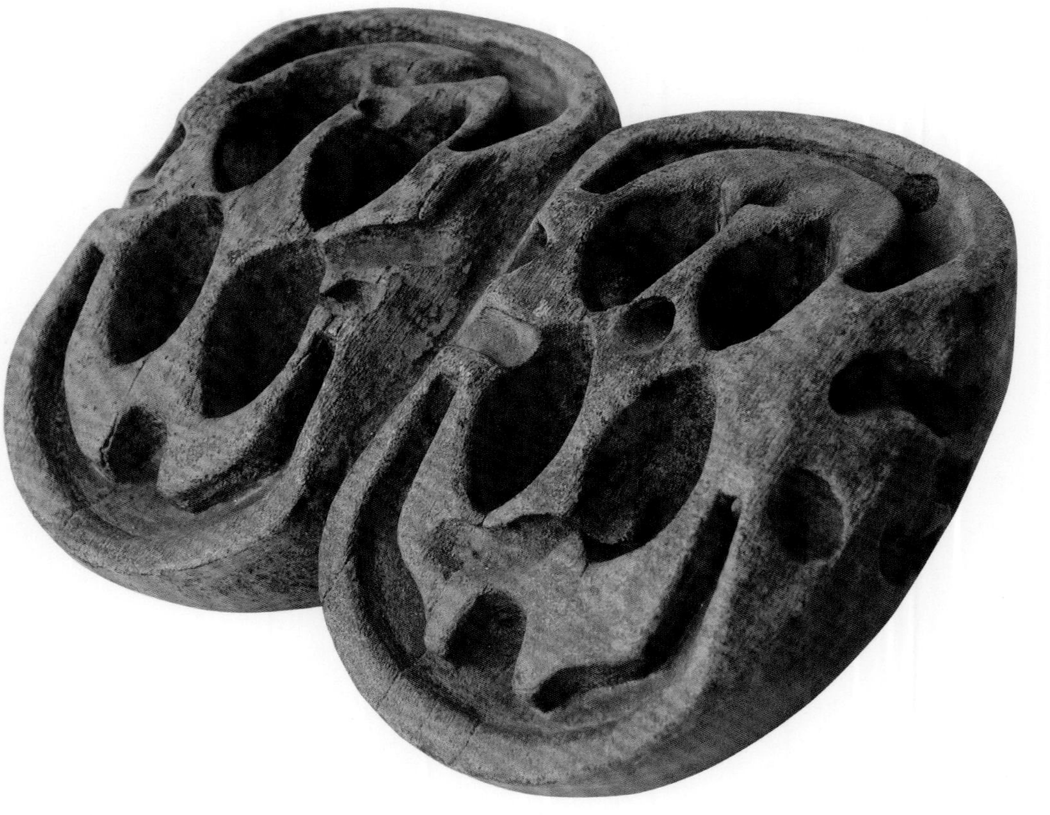

TWINS
連理
Bronze
14.5 x 28 x 25 cm
1970

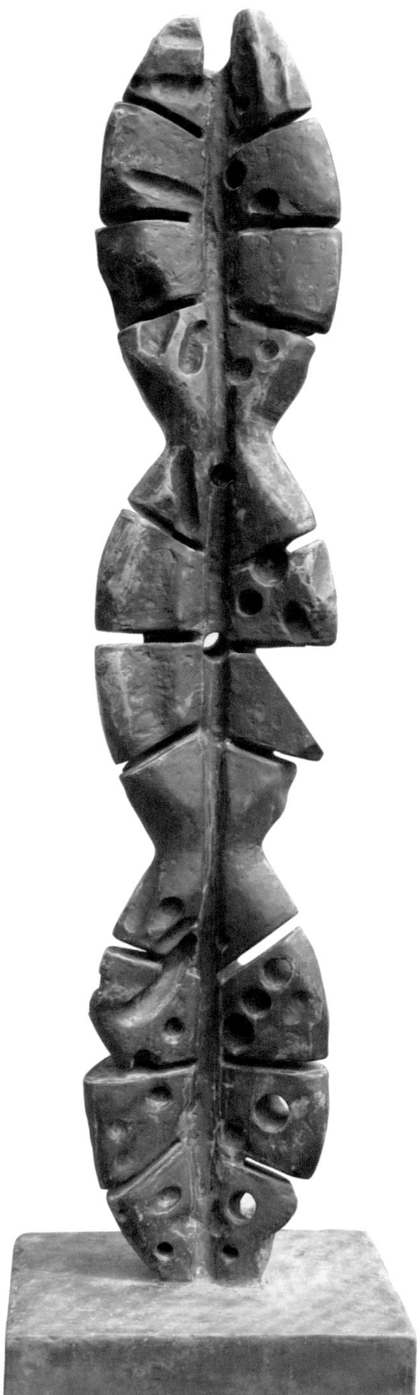

THREE SPIRIT
三奇
Bronze
208 x 55 x 55 cm
1970

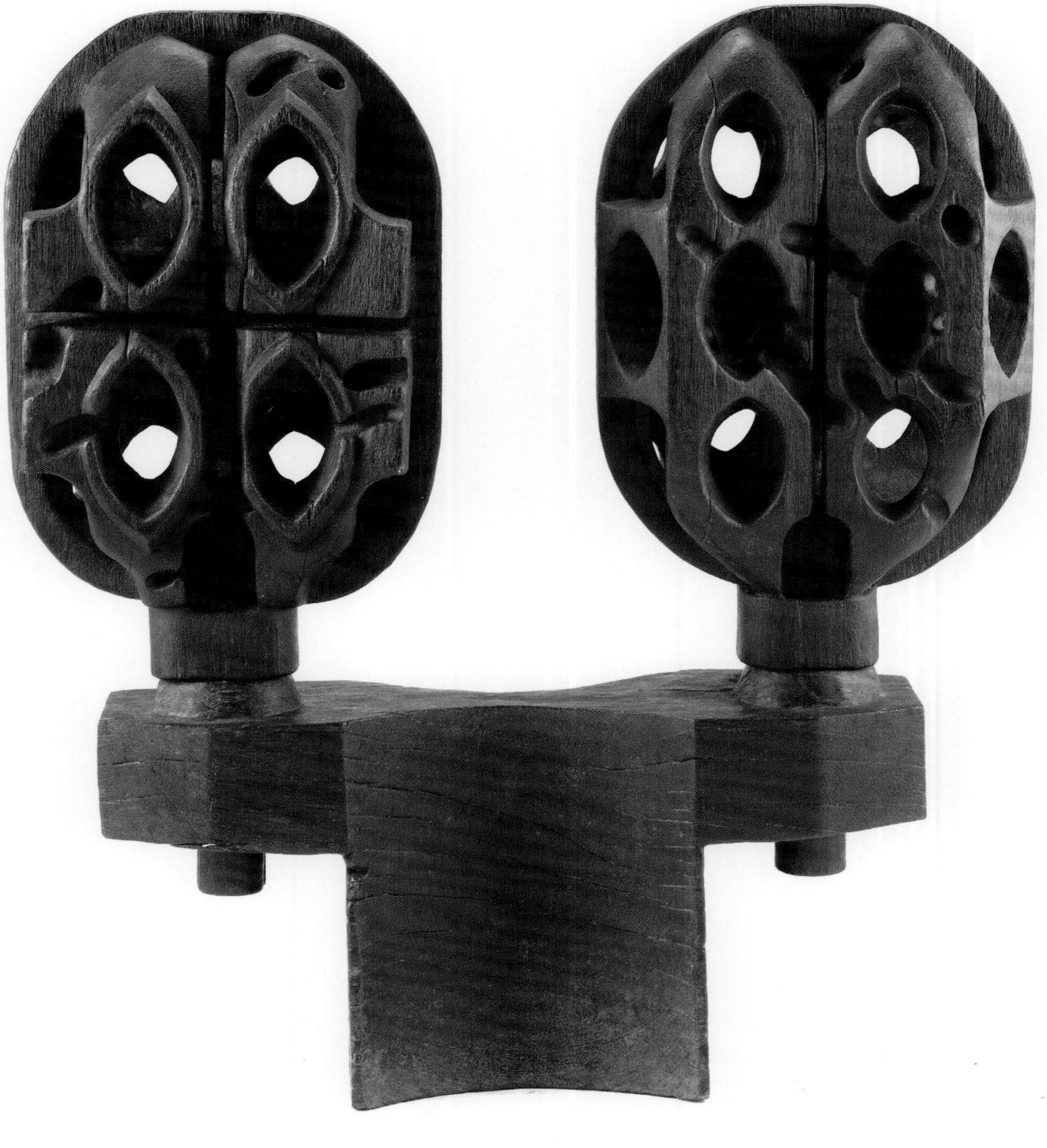

SPIRIT C D
靈丙與丁
Wood/Bronze
75 x 55 cm
1976

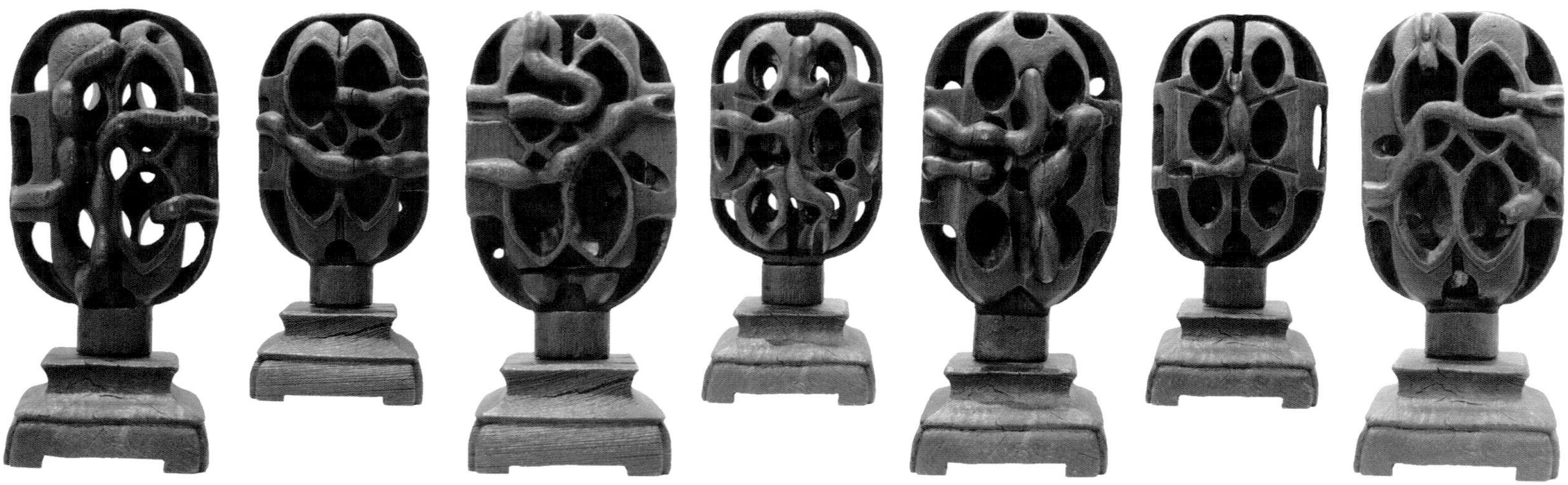

SPIRIT A - G
靈 甲-庚
Bronze
H: 45 cm
1977

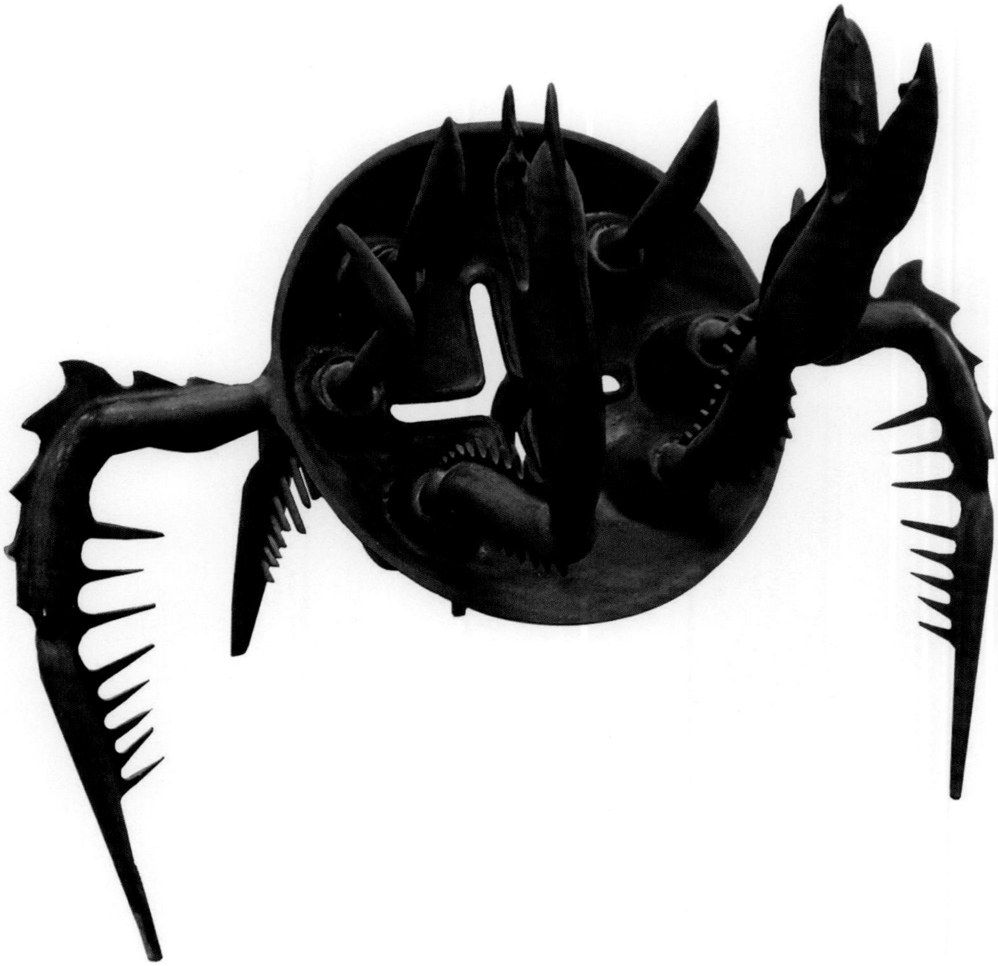

CRAB #4
跛扈將軍#四
Bronze
45 x 59 x 57 cm
1985

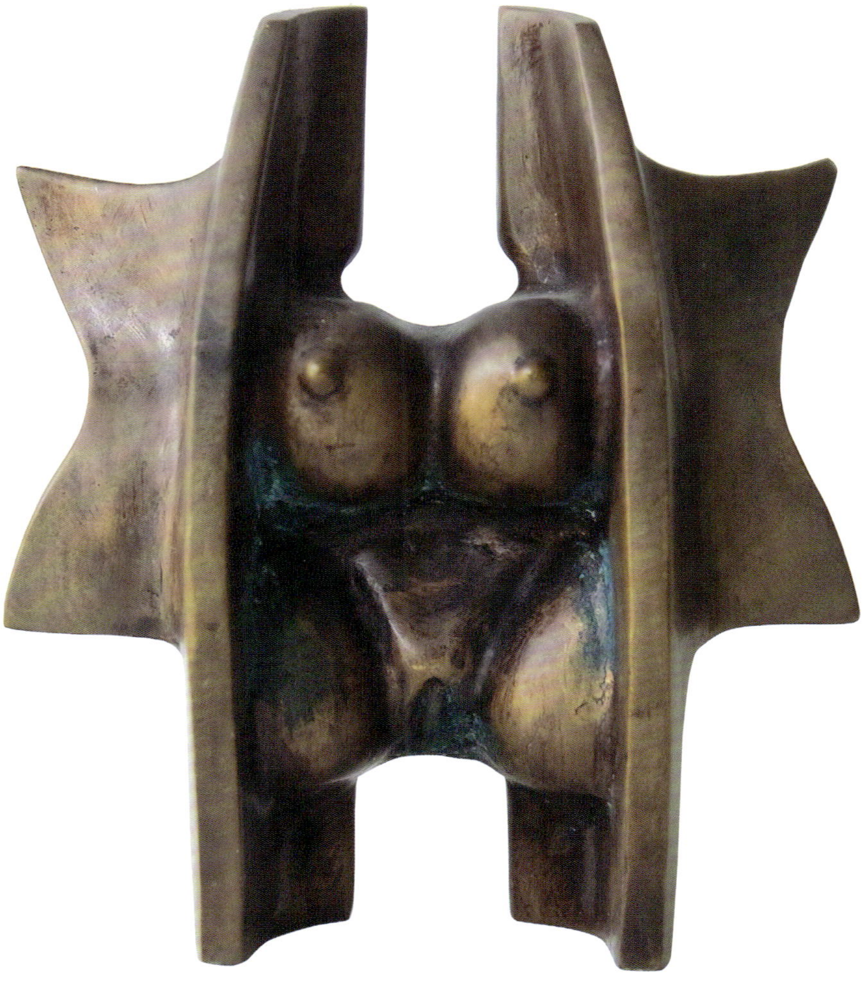

BIRD MAN #1
玄鳥 #一
Bronze
15 x14 x 6.5 cm
1988

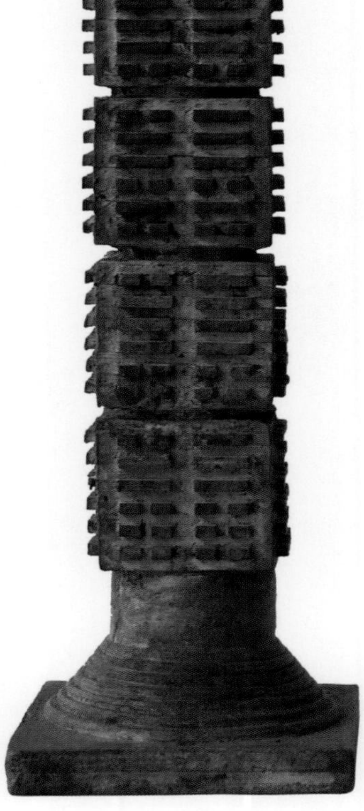

HEAVEN & EARTH
通天
Bronze
34 x 7.5 x 7.5 cm
1992

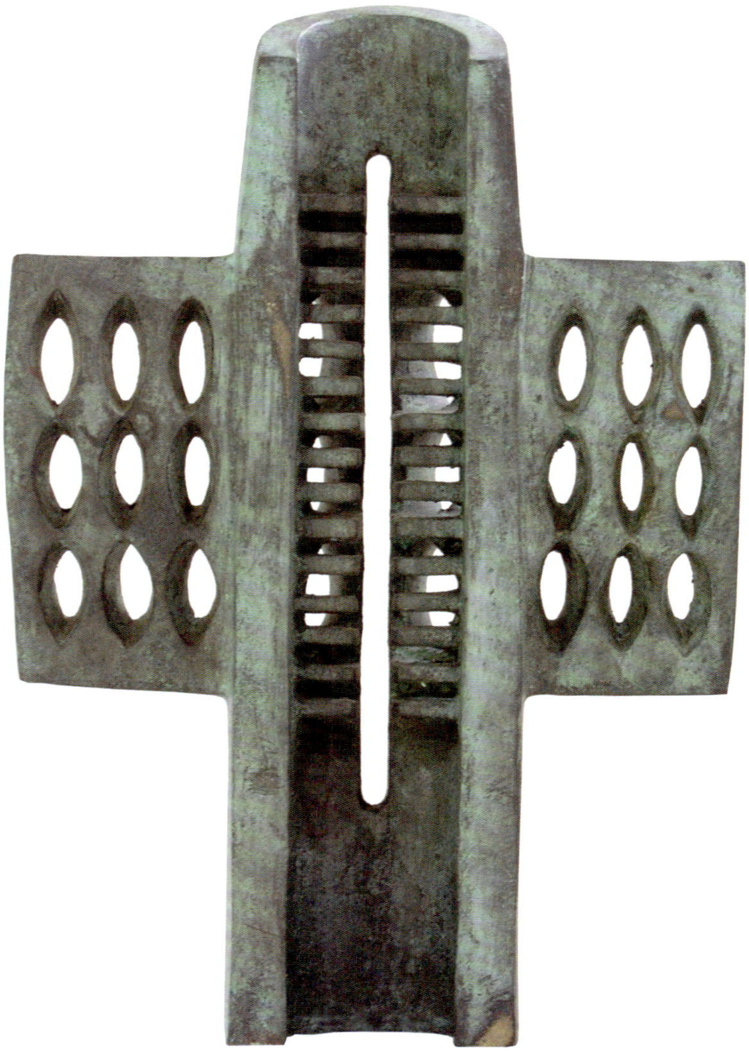

FLYING
翔
Bronze
29 x 19 x 5.5 cm
1992

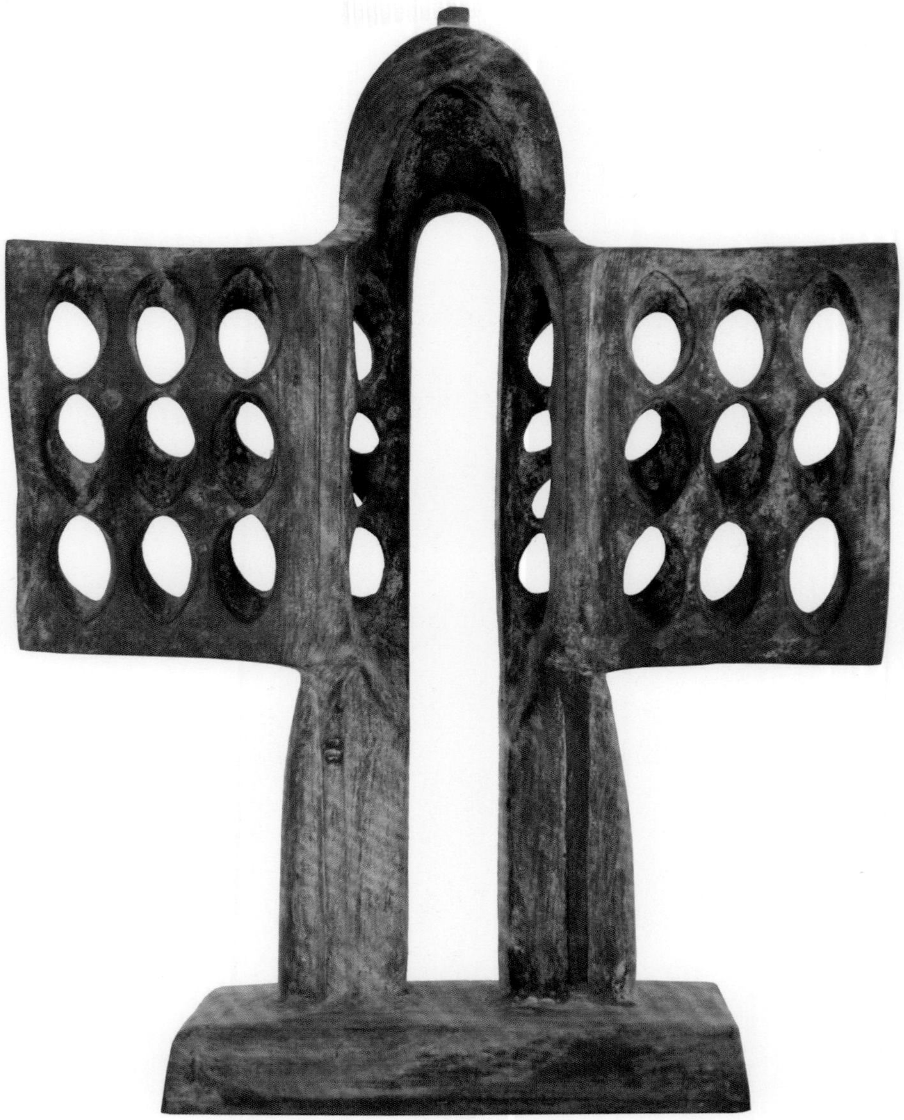

EAGLEMAN
隼人
Bronze
31 x 25 x 11 cm
1992

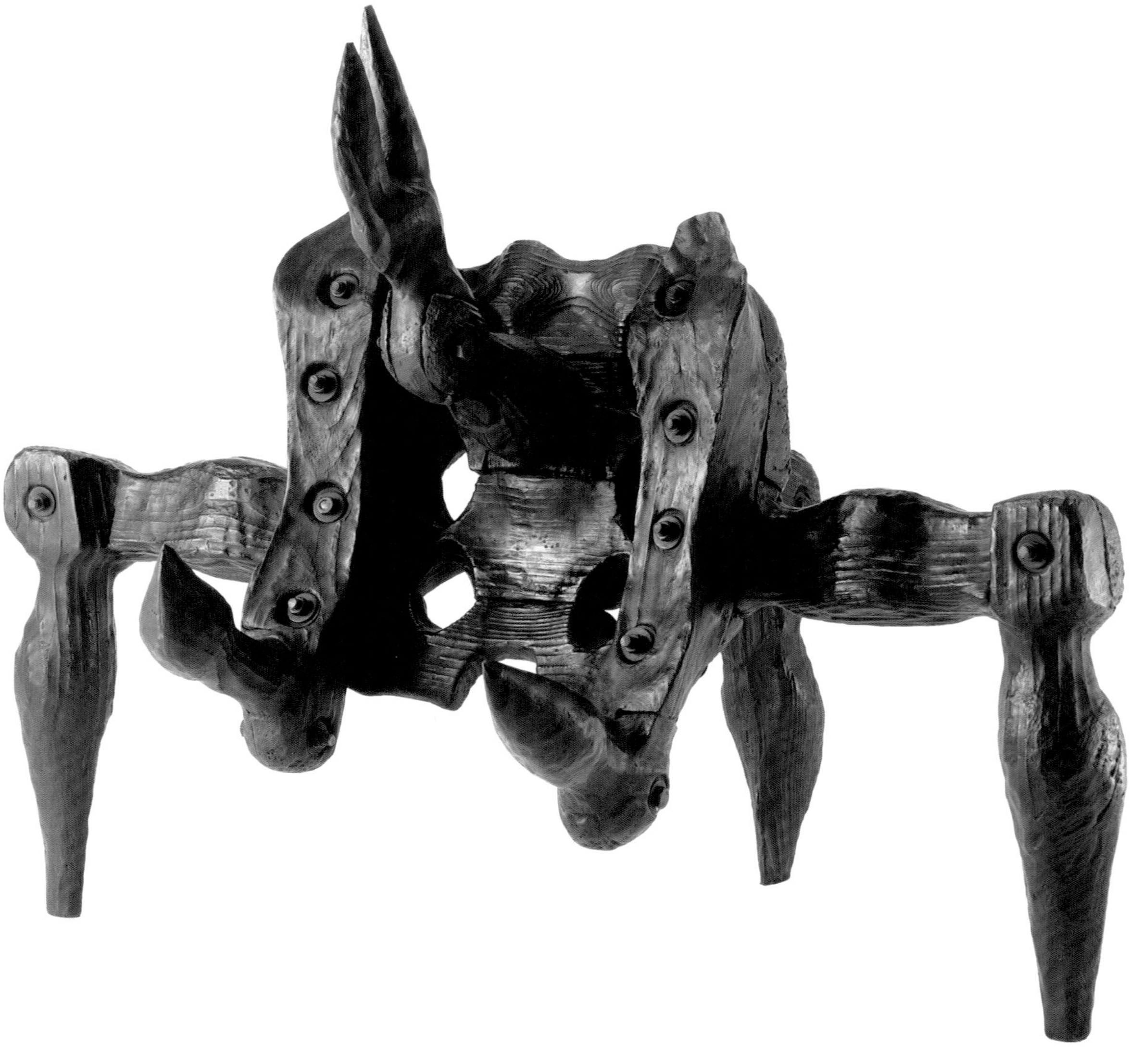

CRAB #5
伏波將軍
Bronze
68 x 65 x 87 cm
1993

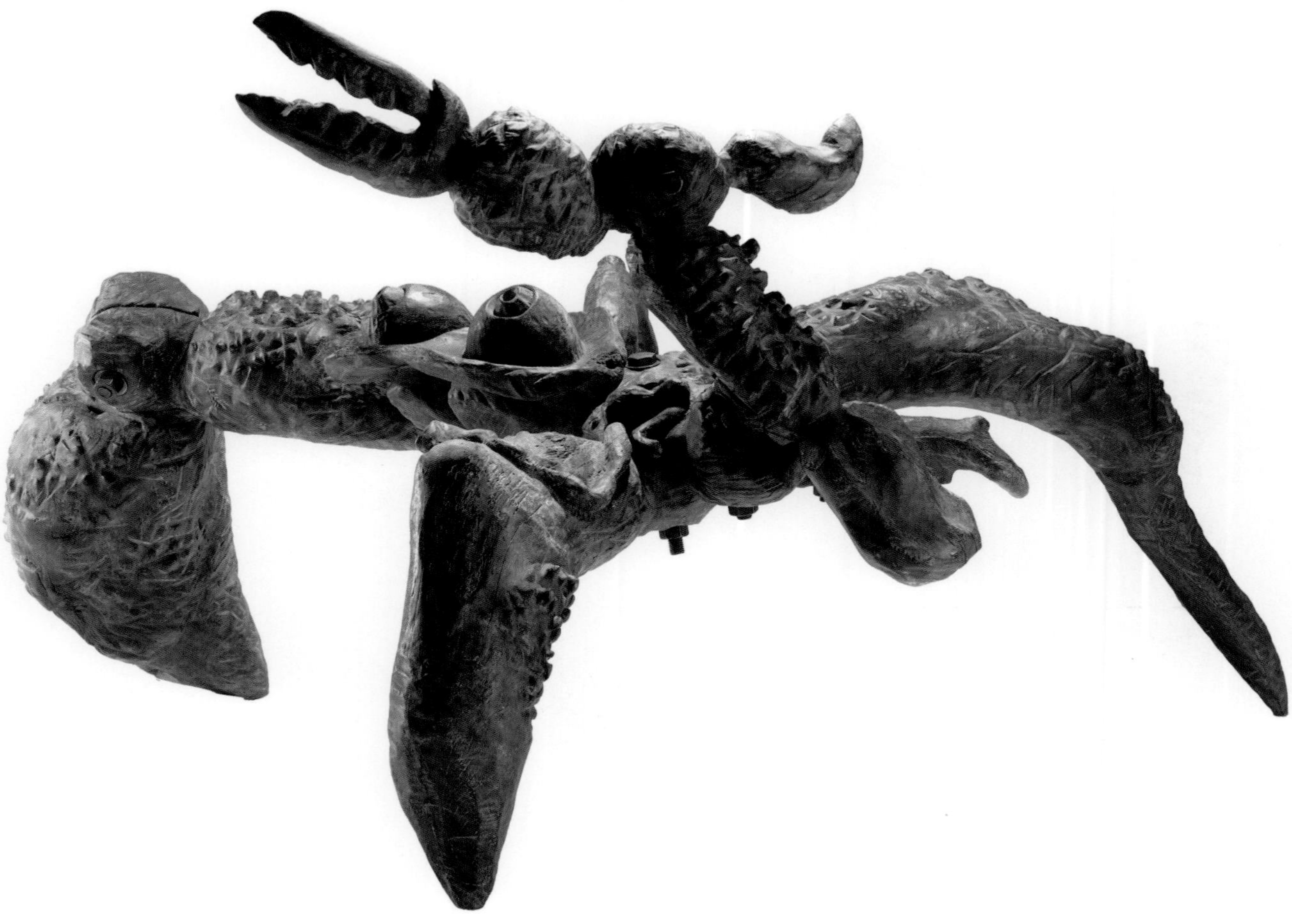

CRAB #6
老驥（橫行萬里）
Wood/Bronze
101 x 110 x 162 cm
1993

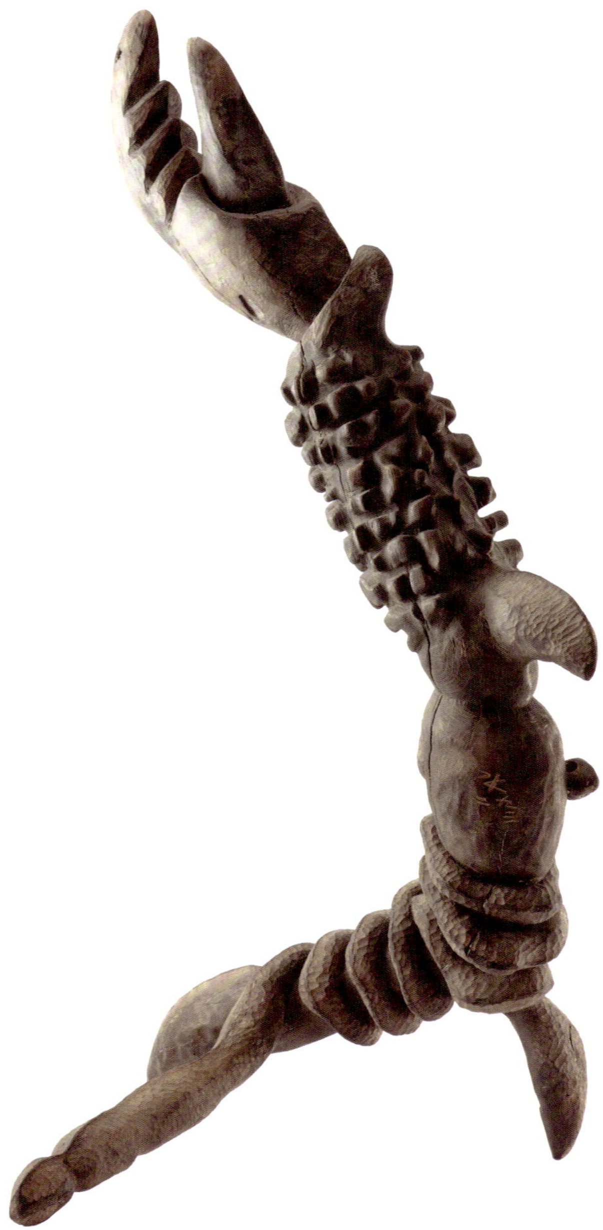

ARMSTRONG
鐵臂
Bronze
H: 83 cm
1993

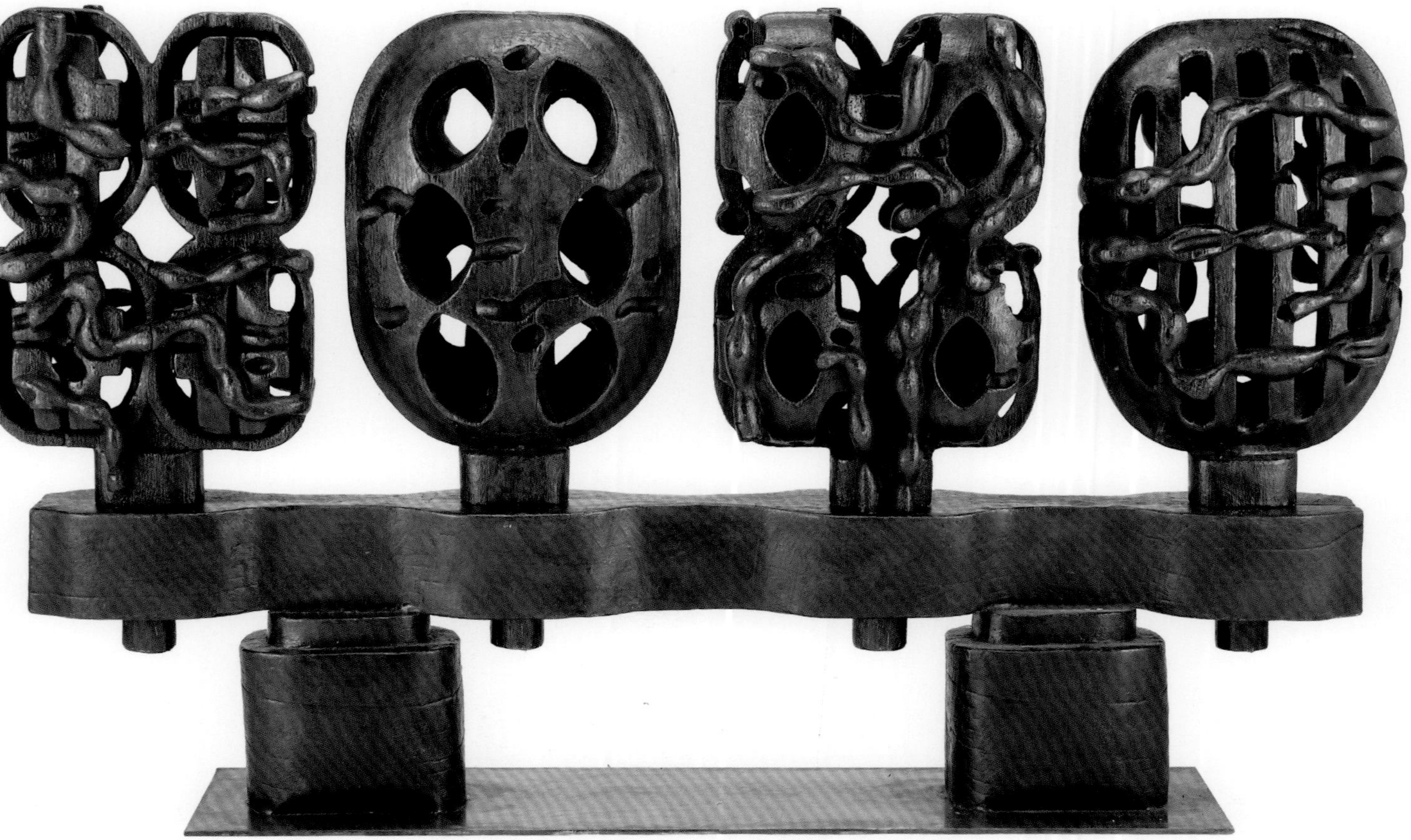

FOUR SPIRIT
四護院
Bronze
74 x 127 x 25 cm
1993

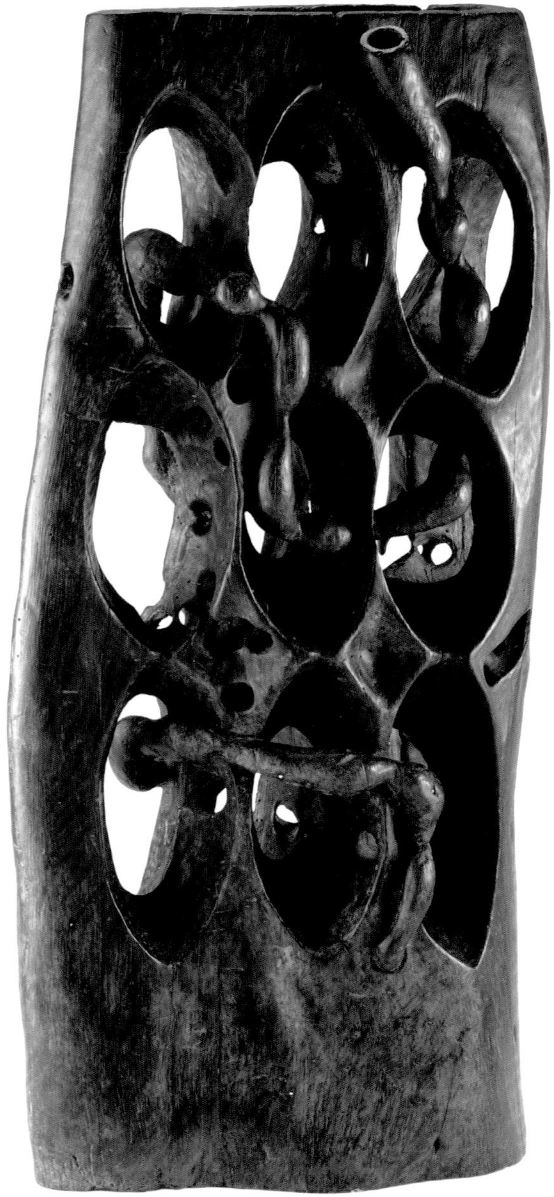

MAGIC NINE
九宮變幻
Bronze
78 x 36 cm
1993

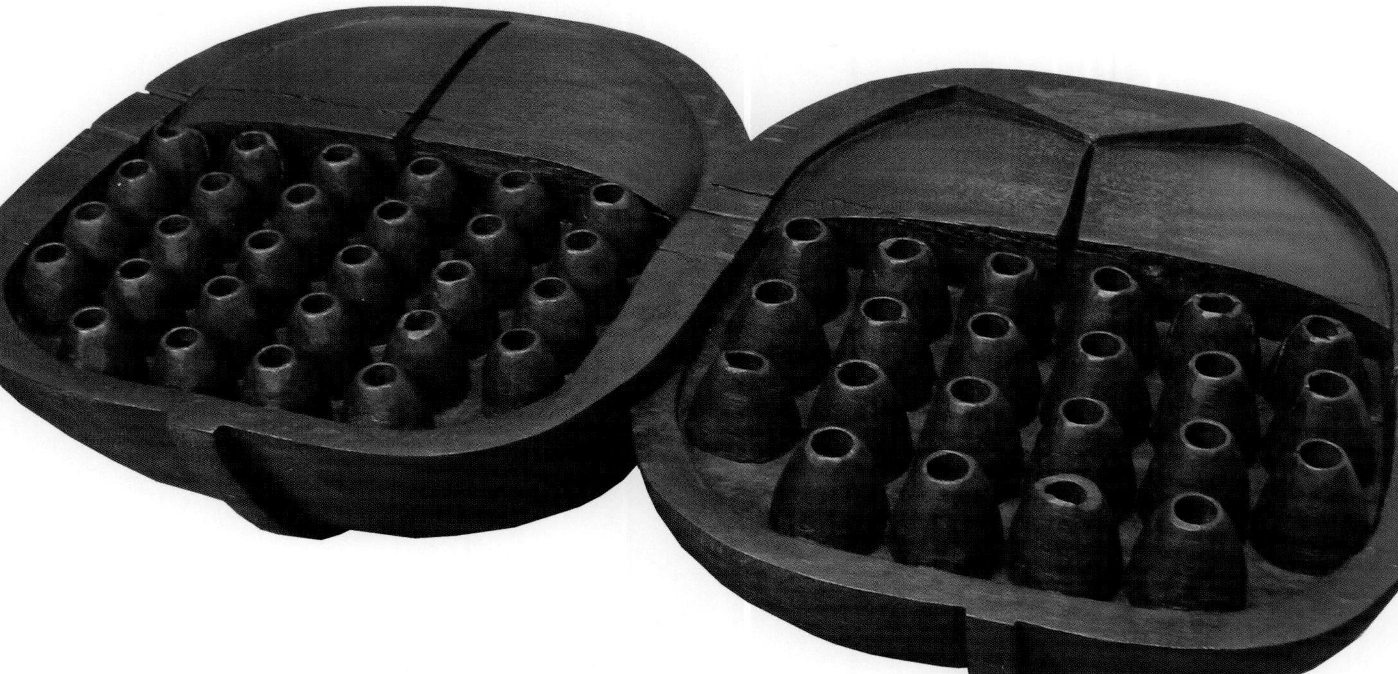

TWINS
連理
Wood
23 x 94 x 52 cm
2007

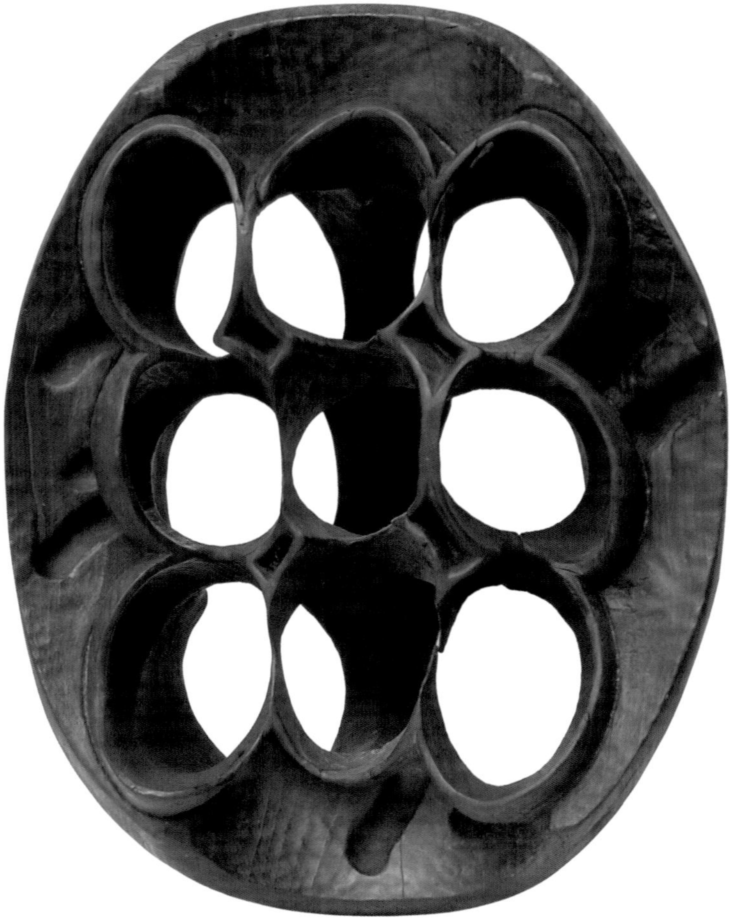

FORTUNE
福
Wood
38 x 51 x 26 cm
1975

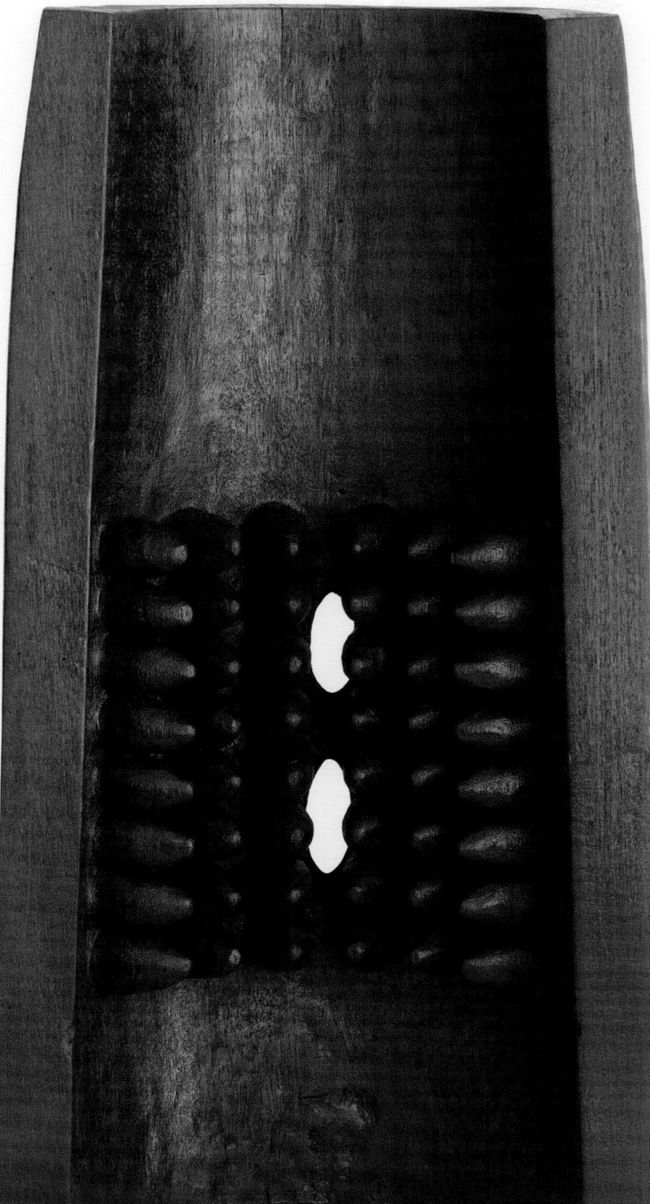

MONOLITH
祖
Wood
54.7 x 29.3 x 15.3 cm
2007

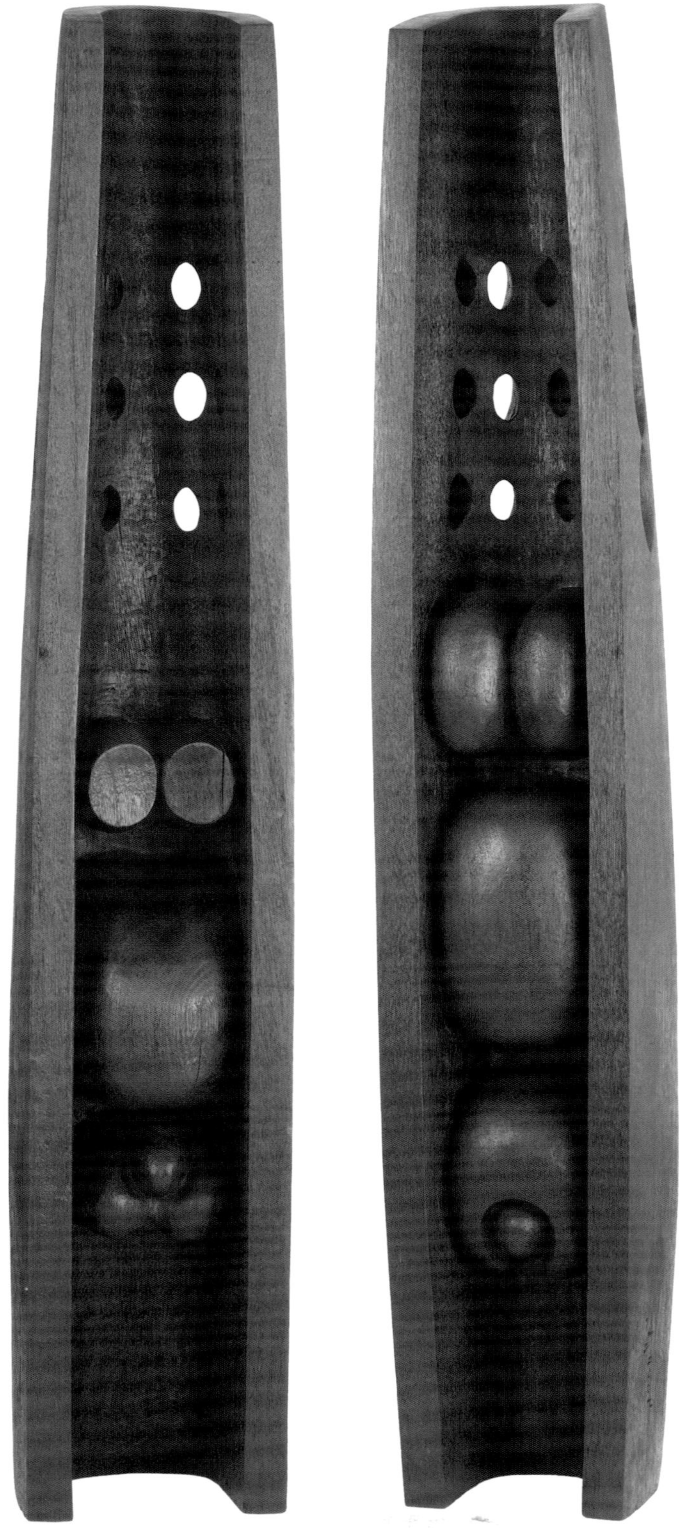

COUPLE
乾坤
Wood
117 x 20.5 x 20.5 cm
2007

Wood Relief
木浮雕

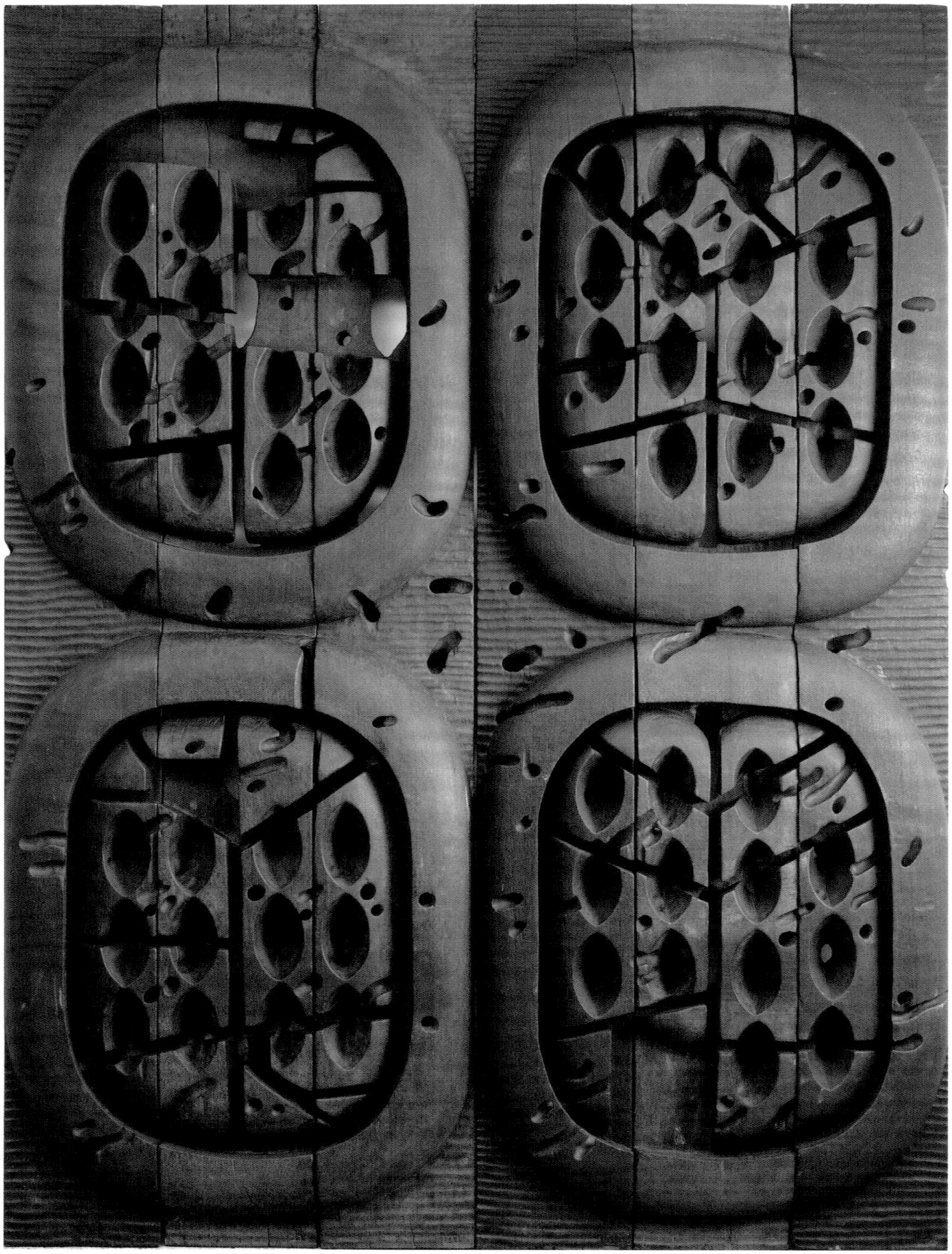

FOUR SPIRITS(FRONT)
四靈（正）
Wood Relief
264 x 183 cm
1975

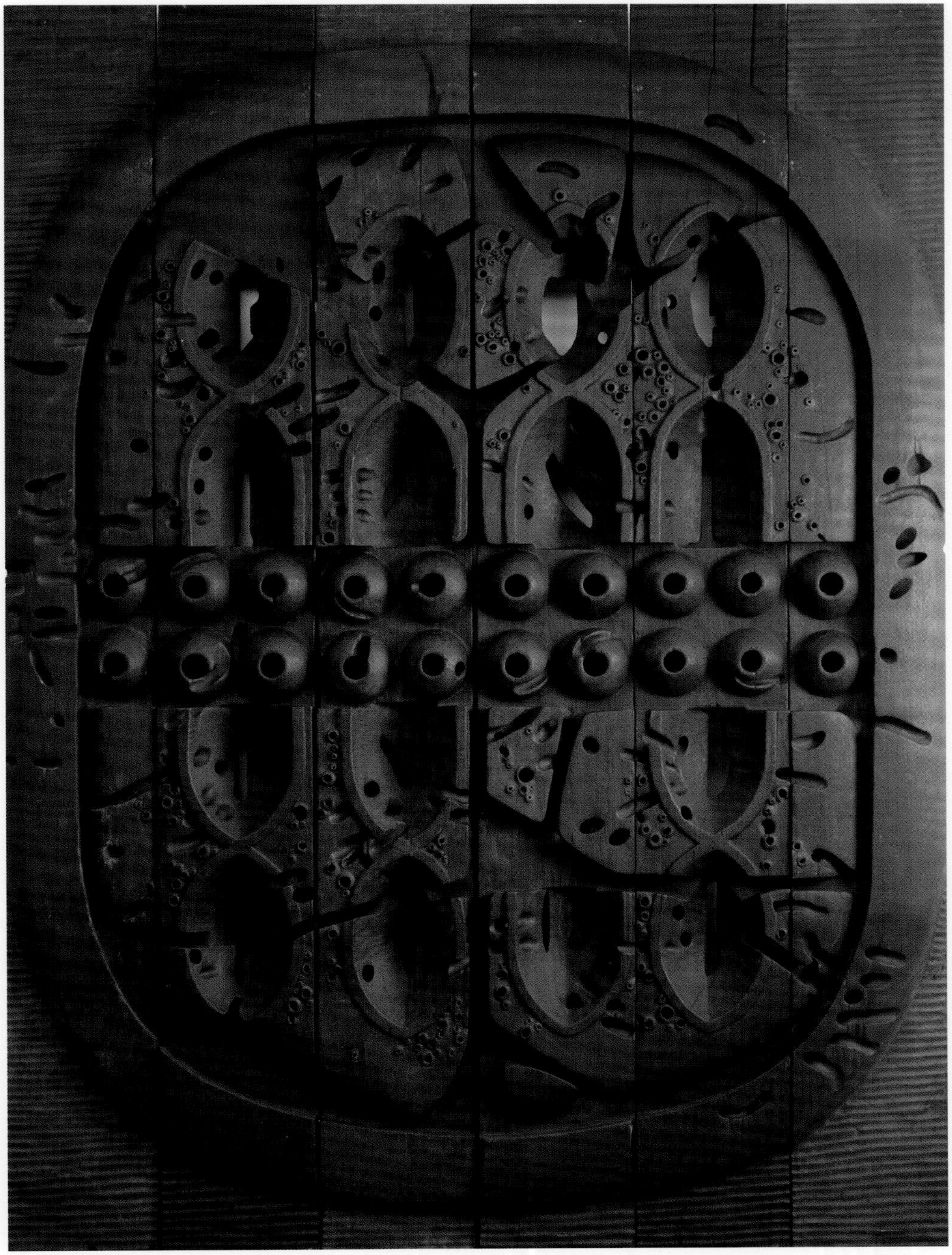

FOUR SPIRITS(BACK)
四靈（背）
Wood Relief
264 x 183 cm
1975

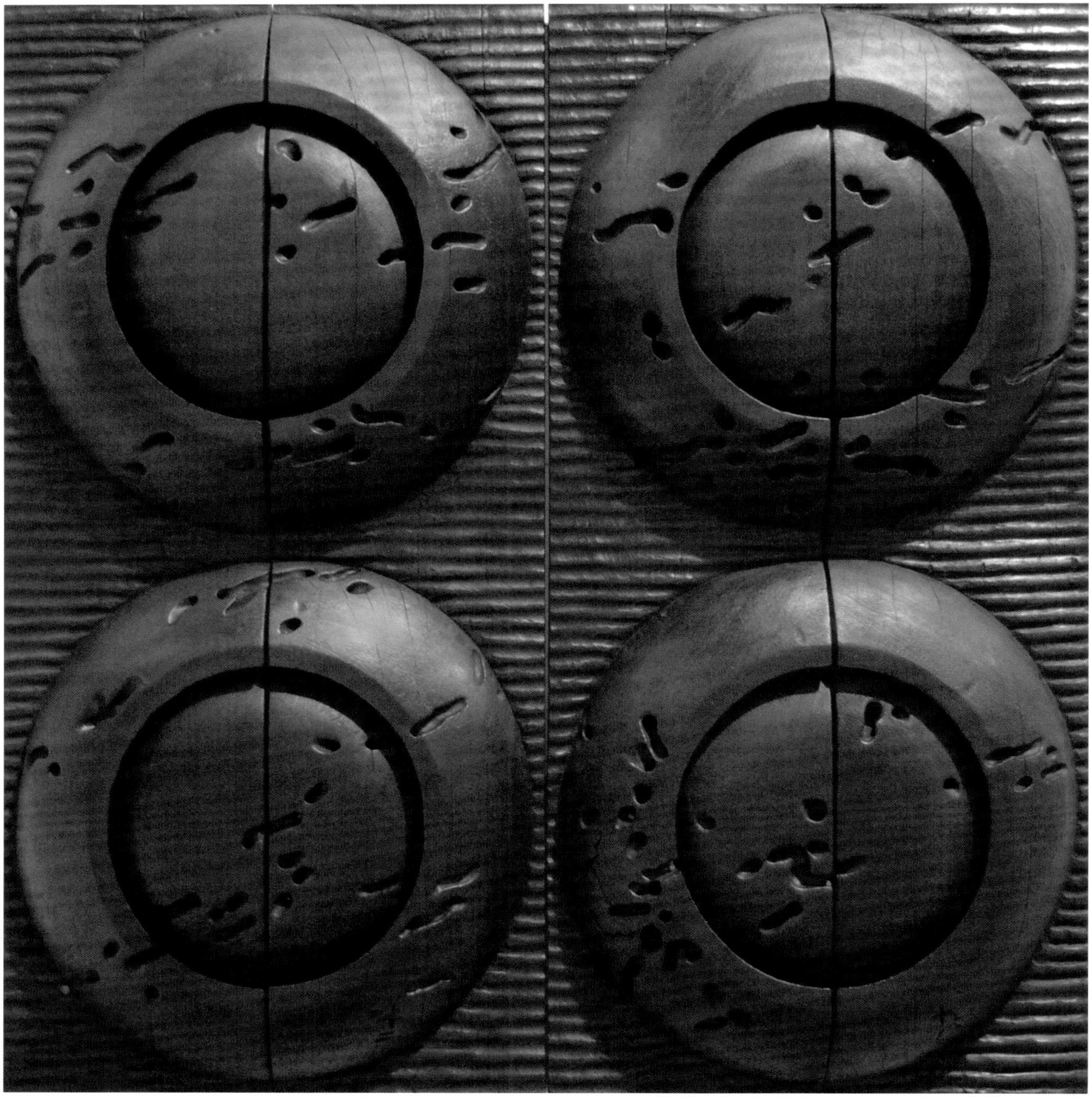

EARTH
大地
Wood Relief
122 x 122 x 10 cm
1998

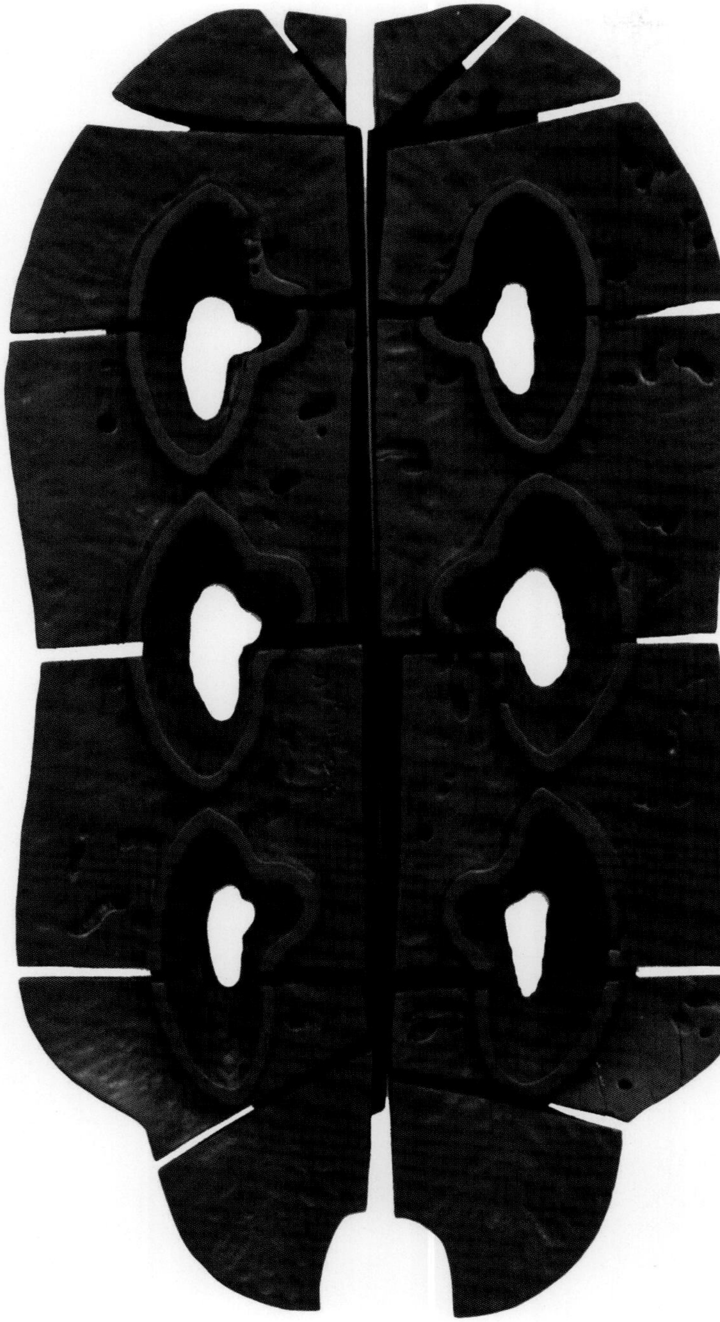

FORTUNE
富
Wood Relief
108 x 60 x 10 cm
2006

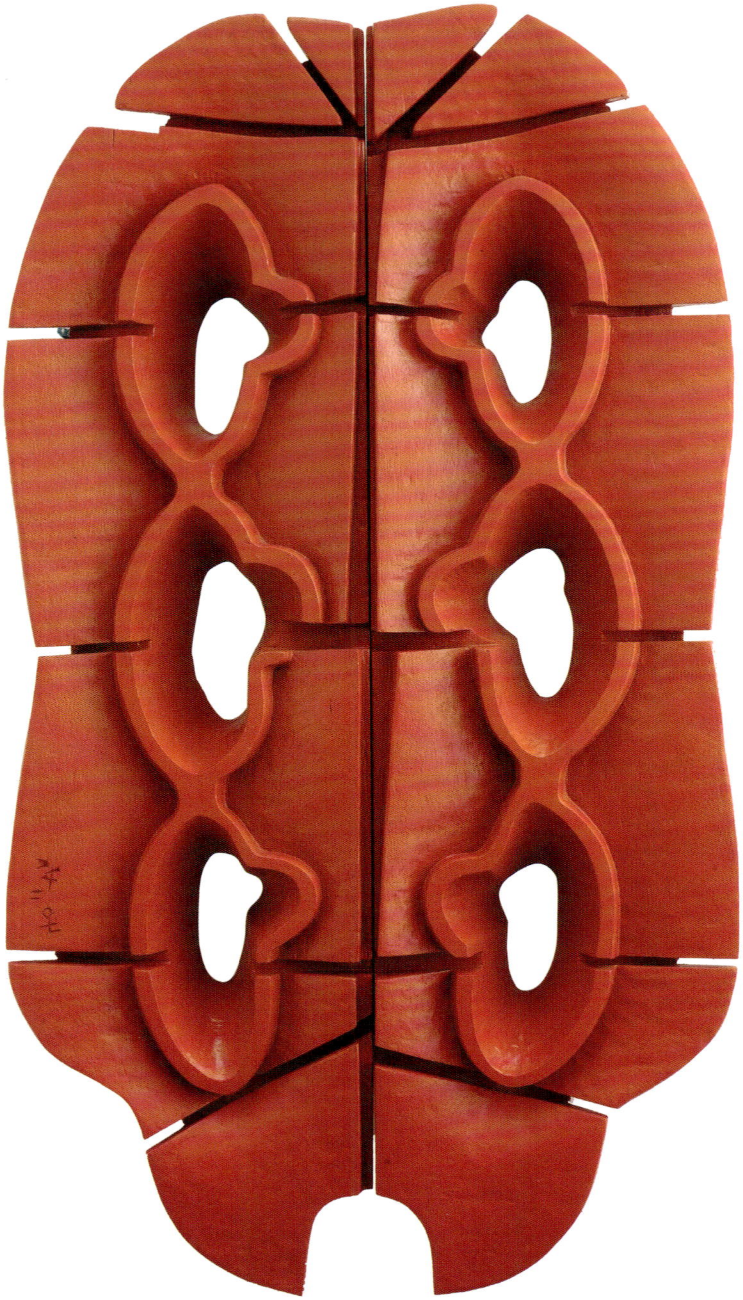

FORTUNE SIX
六合
Wood Relief
108 x 60 x 10 cm
2007

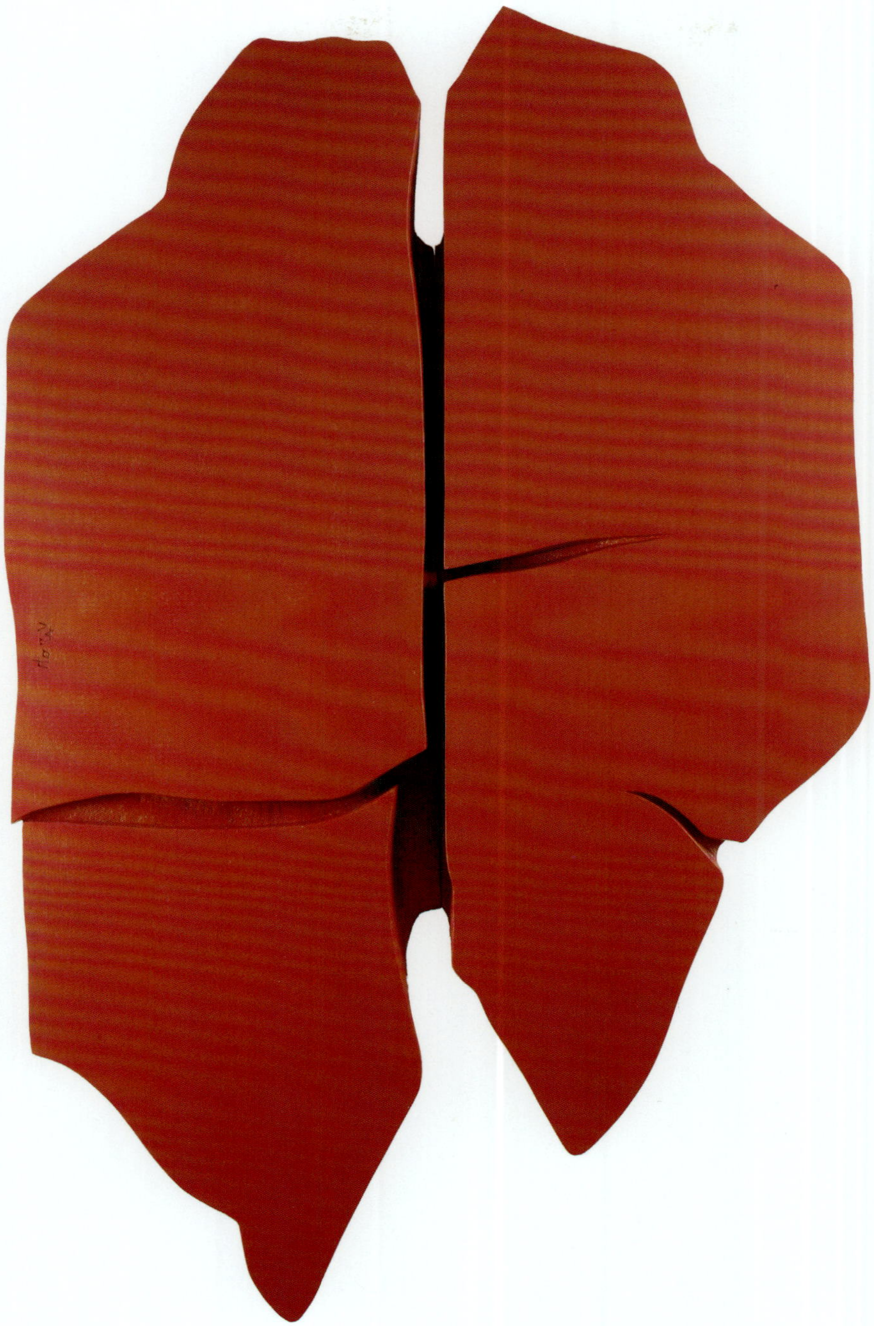

FORTUNE
福
Wood Relief
104 x 81 x 7.5 cm
2007

FORTUNE
福
Wood Relief
104 x 81 x 7.5 cm
2007

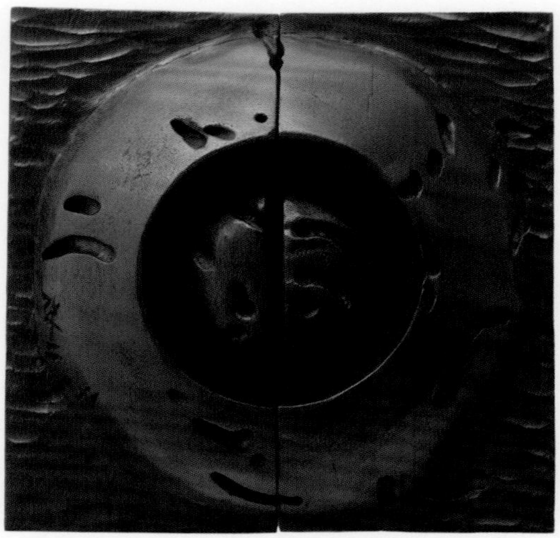

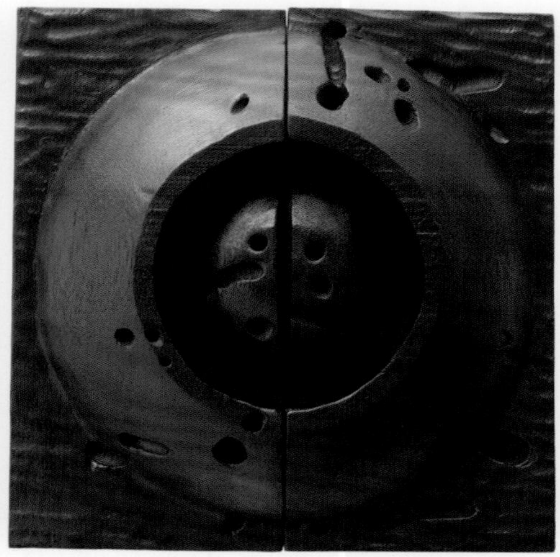

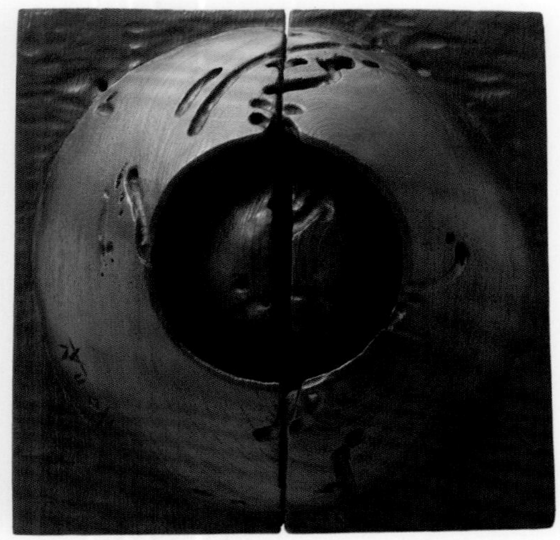

CIRCLE # 1
圓 #一
Wood Relief
29 x 29 x 7 cm
2007

CIRCLE # 2
圓 #二
Wood Relief
29 x 29 x 7 cm
2007

CIRCLE # 3
圓 #三
Wood Relief
31 x 31 x 11 cm
2007

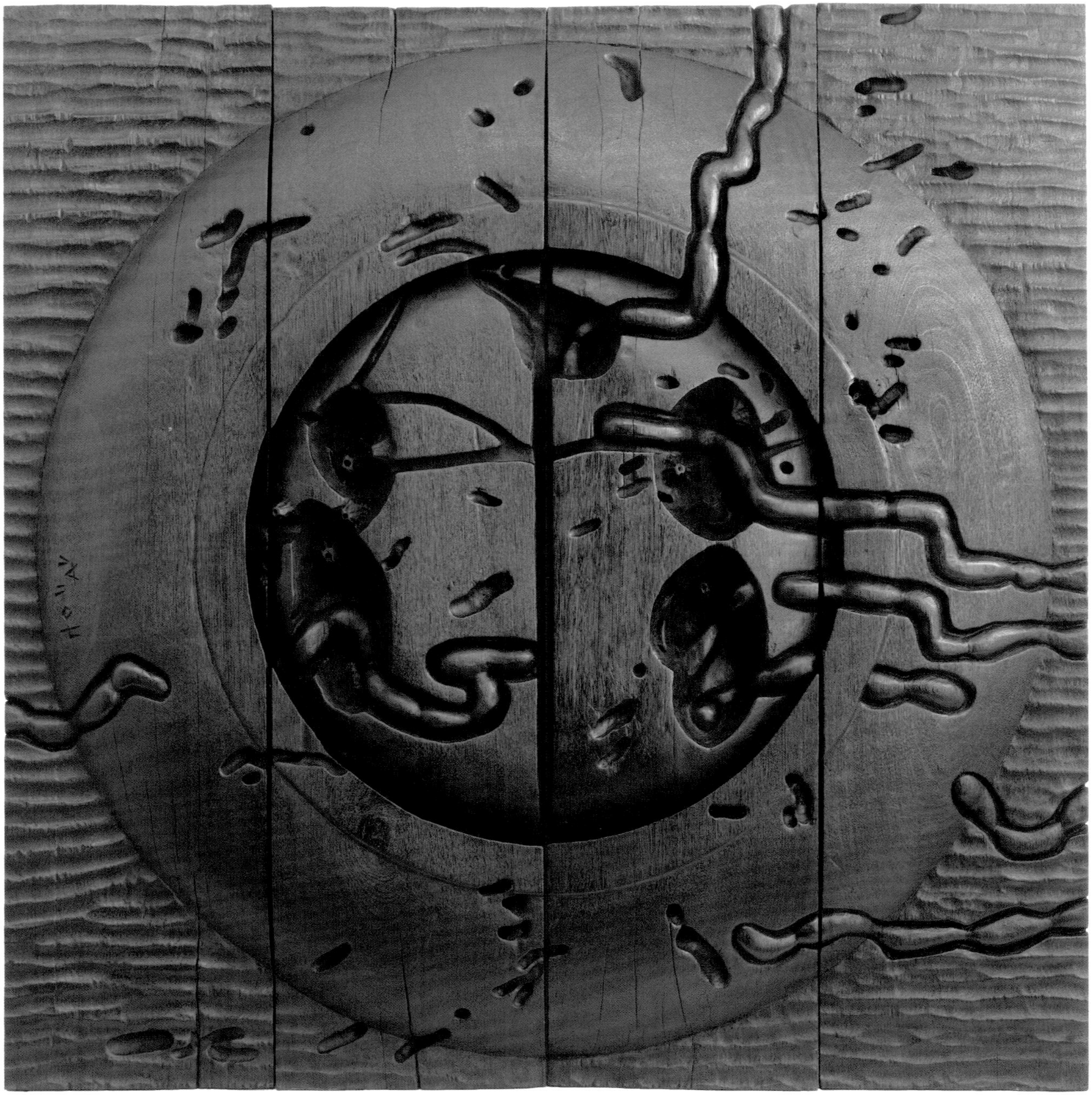

GENESIS
原
Wood Relief
122 x 122 x 10 cm
2007

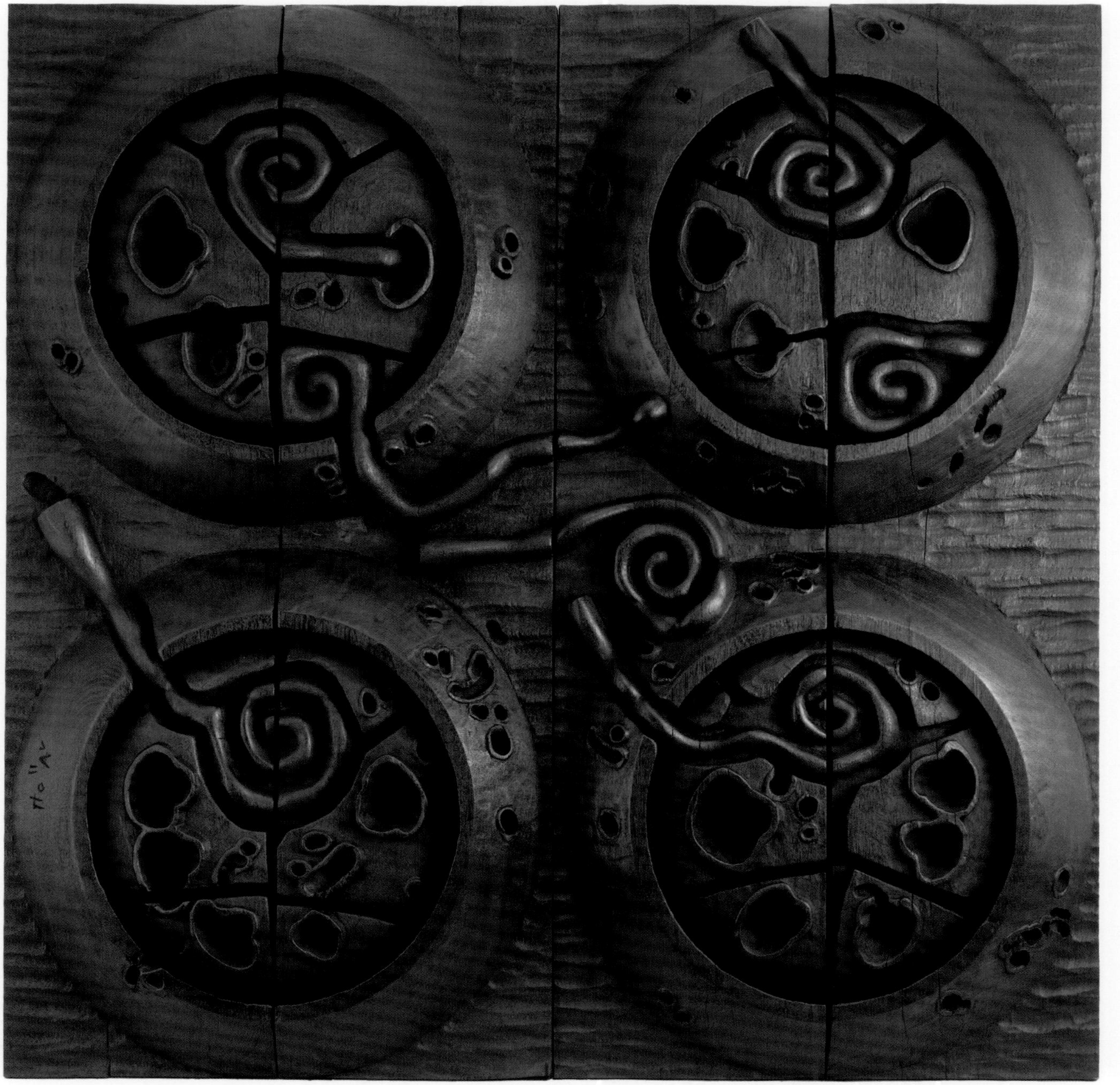

FOUR CIRCLES
四宮
Wood Relief
122 x 122 x 10 cm
2007

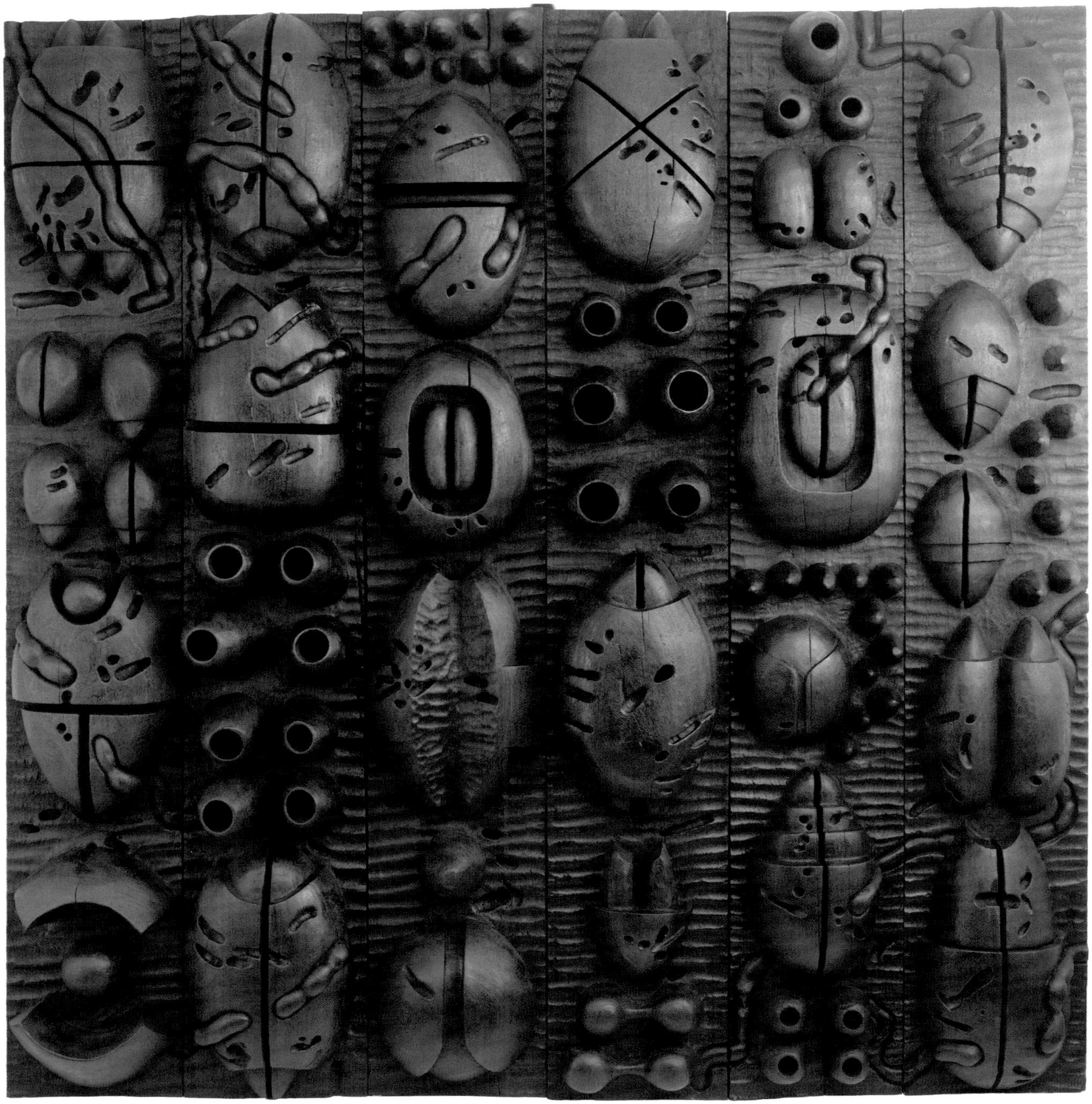

TABLET
銘
Wood Relief
183 x 183 x 15 cm
2007

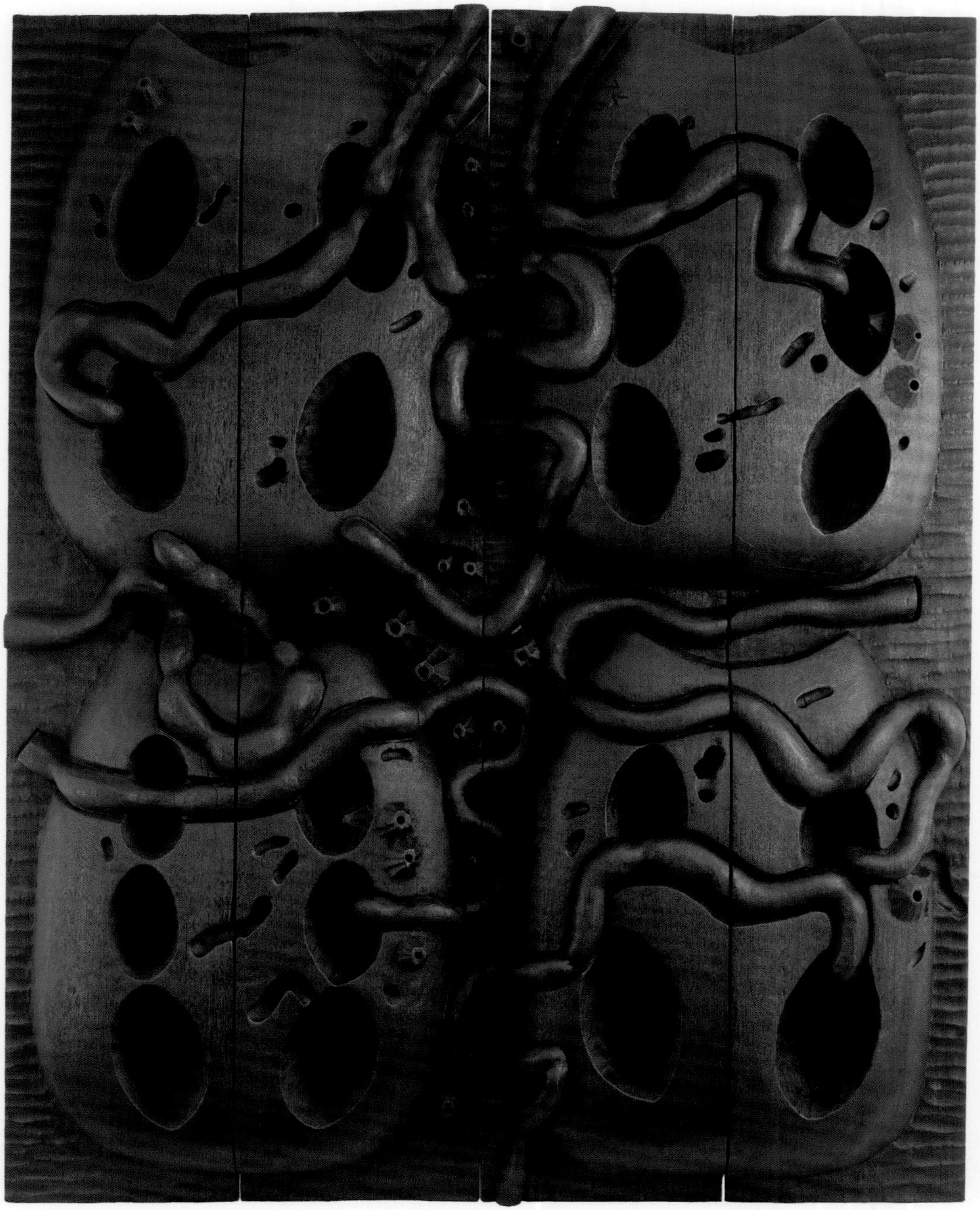

FORTUNE FOUR
方福
Wood Relief
152 x 122 x 15 cm
2007

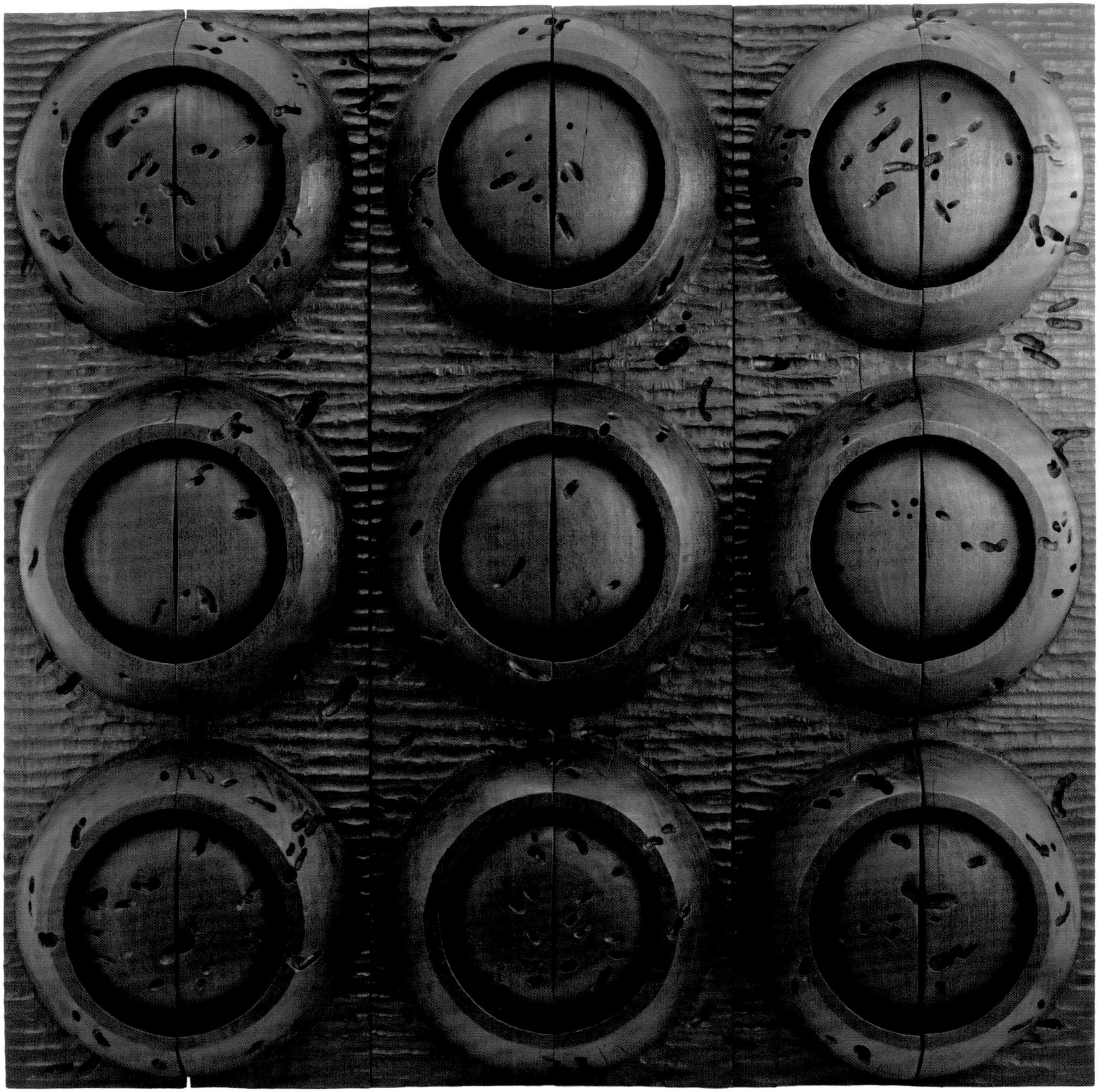

MAGIC SQUARE
九宫
Wood Relief
183 x 183 x 15 cm
2007

Cast Paper
鑄紙

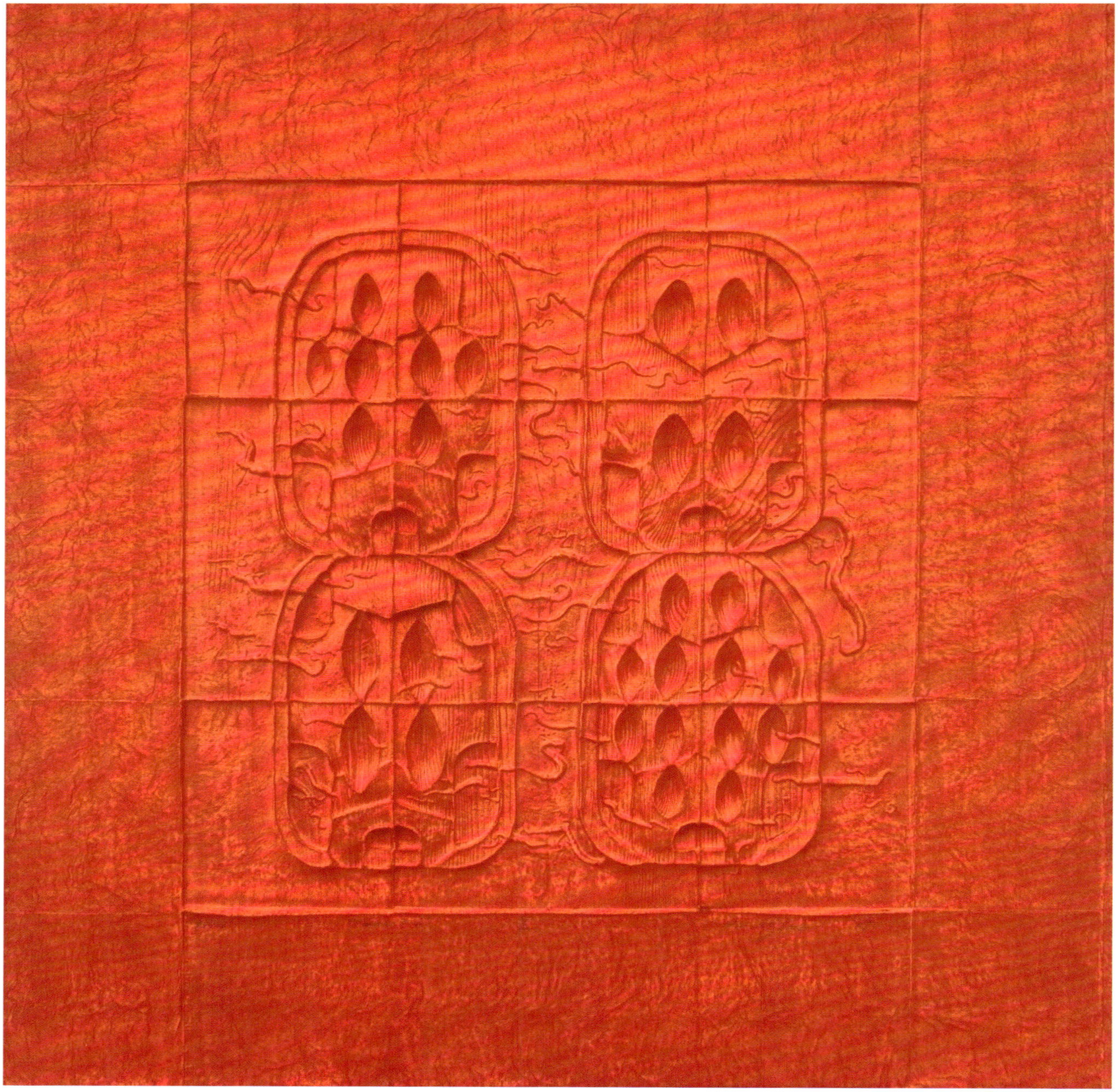

951128 FORTUNE 4
富
Cast Paper on Wood
92 x 91 cm
1995

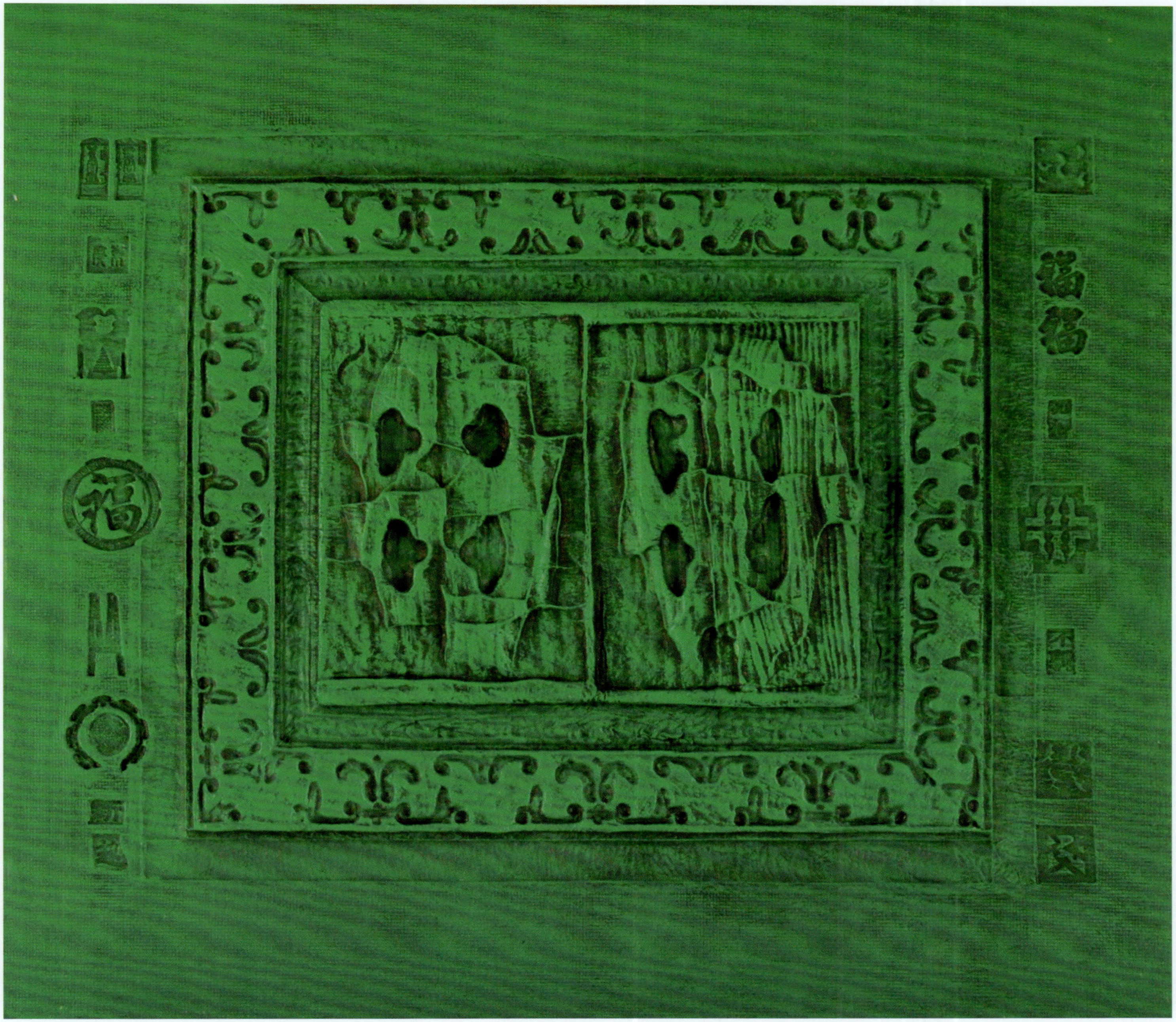

030319 TWIN FORTUNE
雙福
Cast Paper on Wood
48 x 53 cm
1999

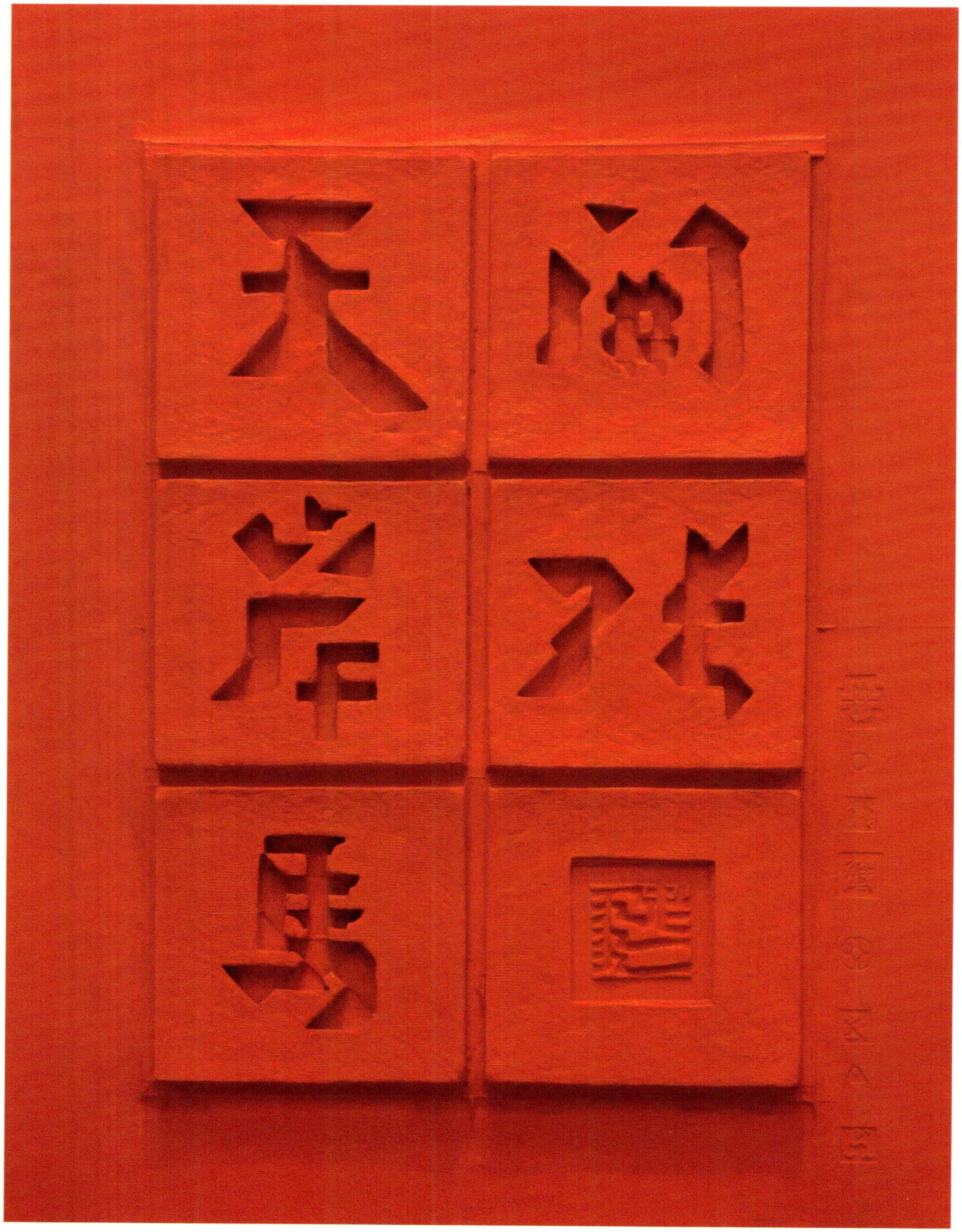

990728 SKY HORSE
天岸馬
Cast Paper on Wood
91 x 71 cm
1999

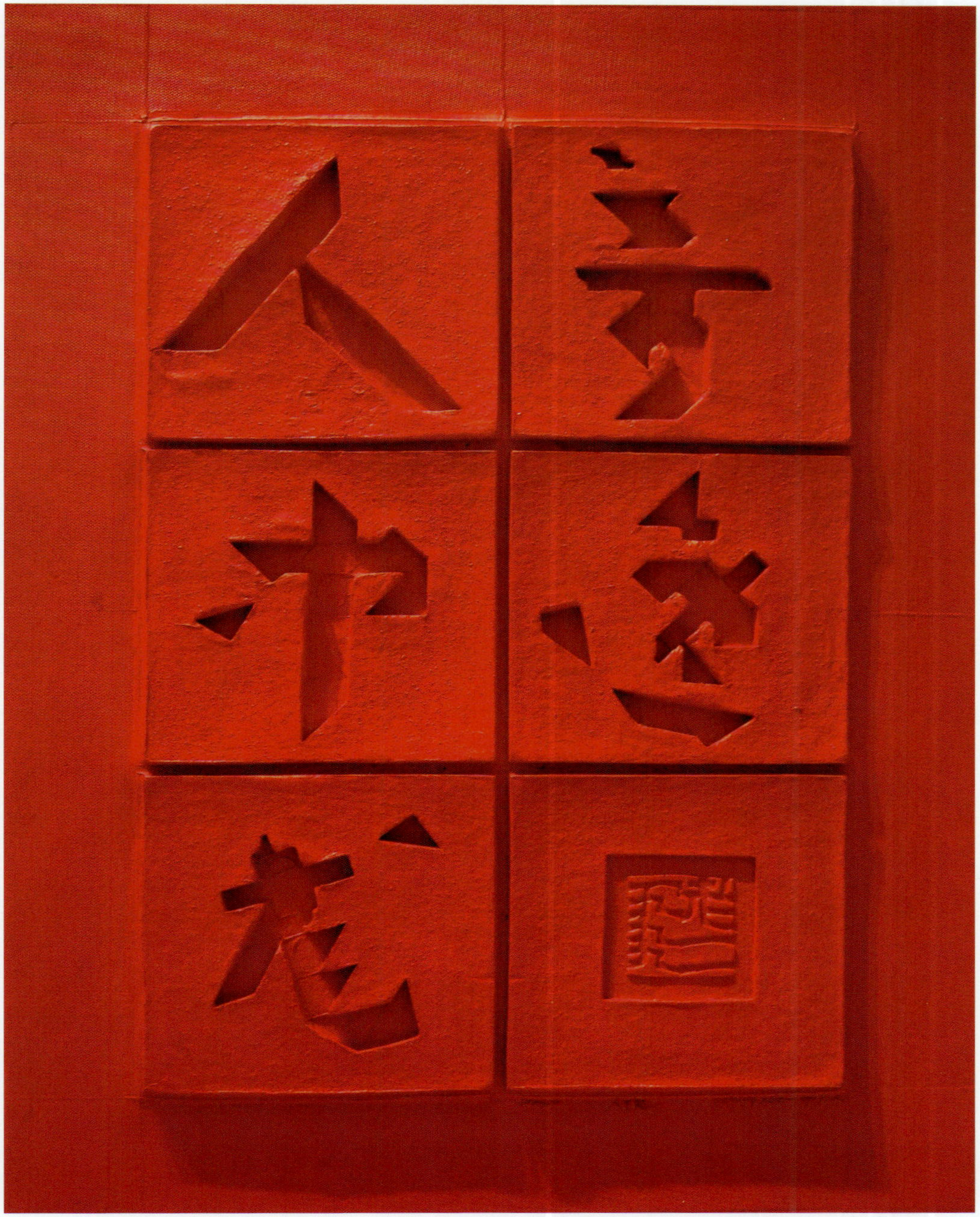

990712 DRAGON
人中龍
Cast Paper on Wood
92 x 71.5 cm
1999

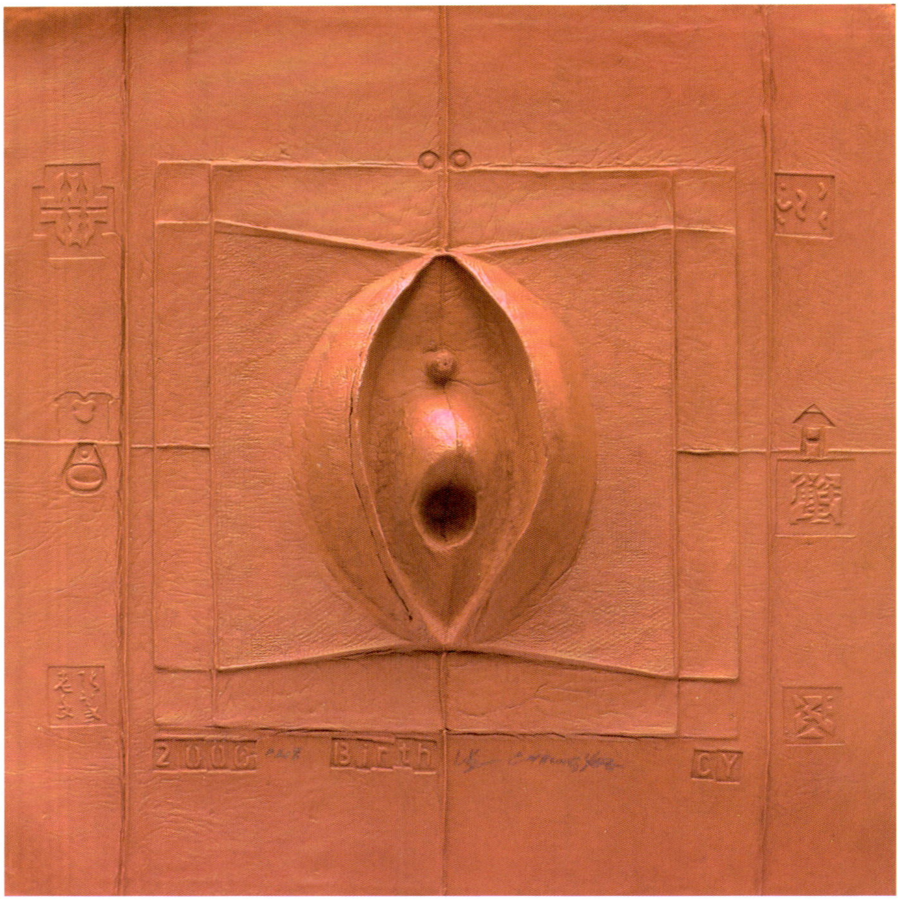

00218 BIRTH
生
Cast Paper in Frame
41 x 41 cm
1999

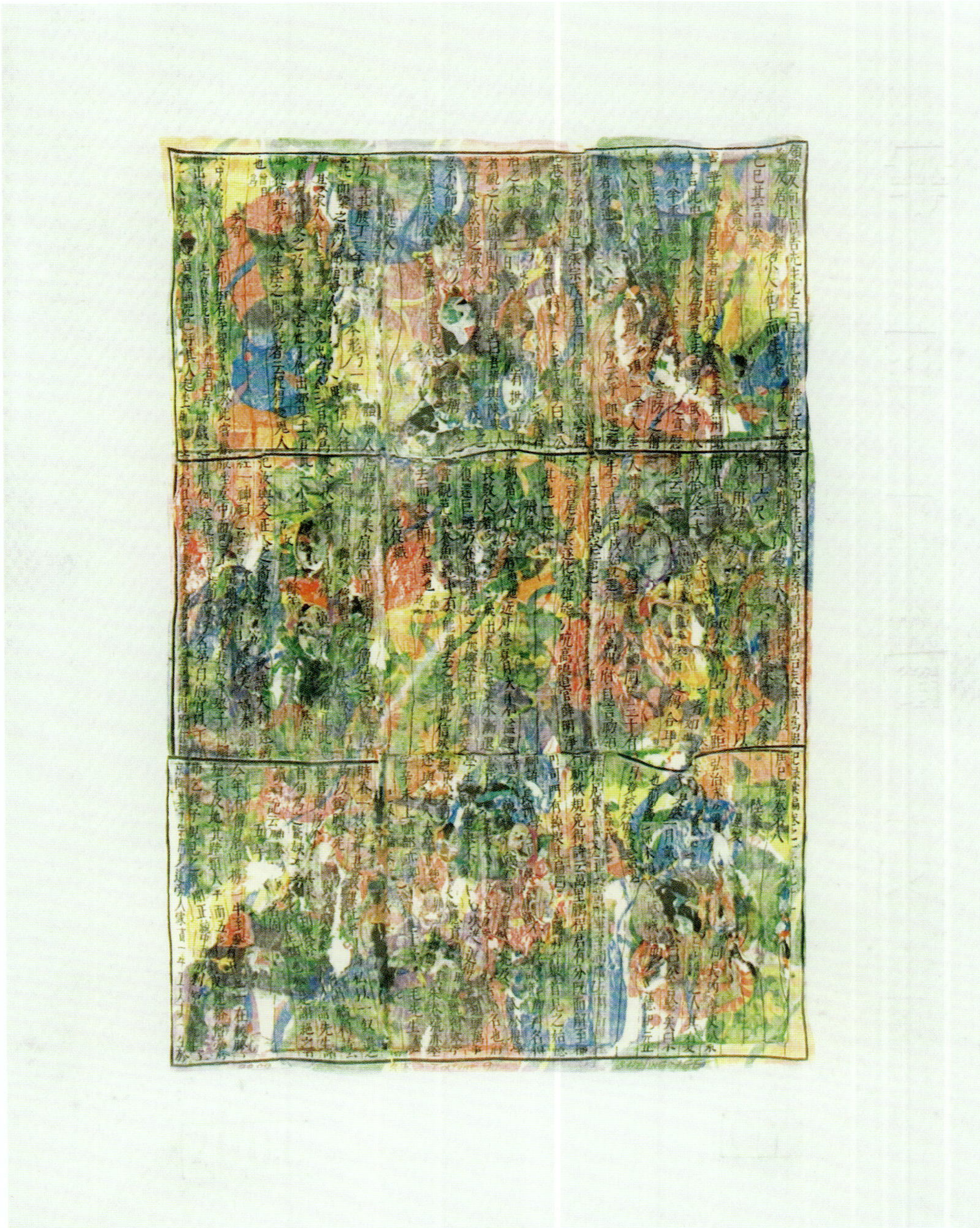

0209 FORTUNE 9
久富
Cast Paper on Wood
66 x 51 cm
2000

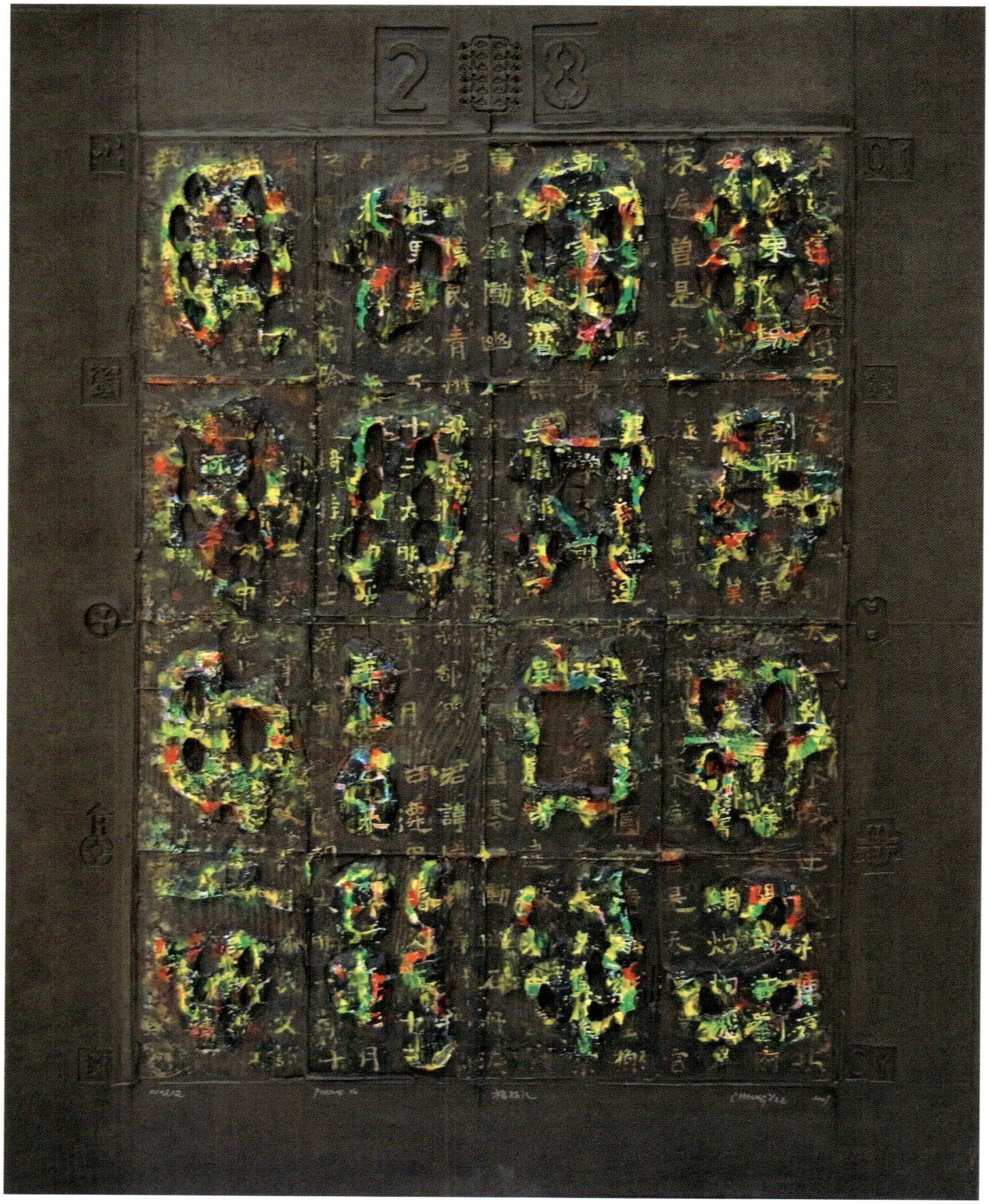

010212 FORTUNE 16
富孖八
Cast Paper on Wood
92 x 72 cm
2001

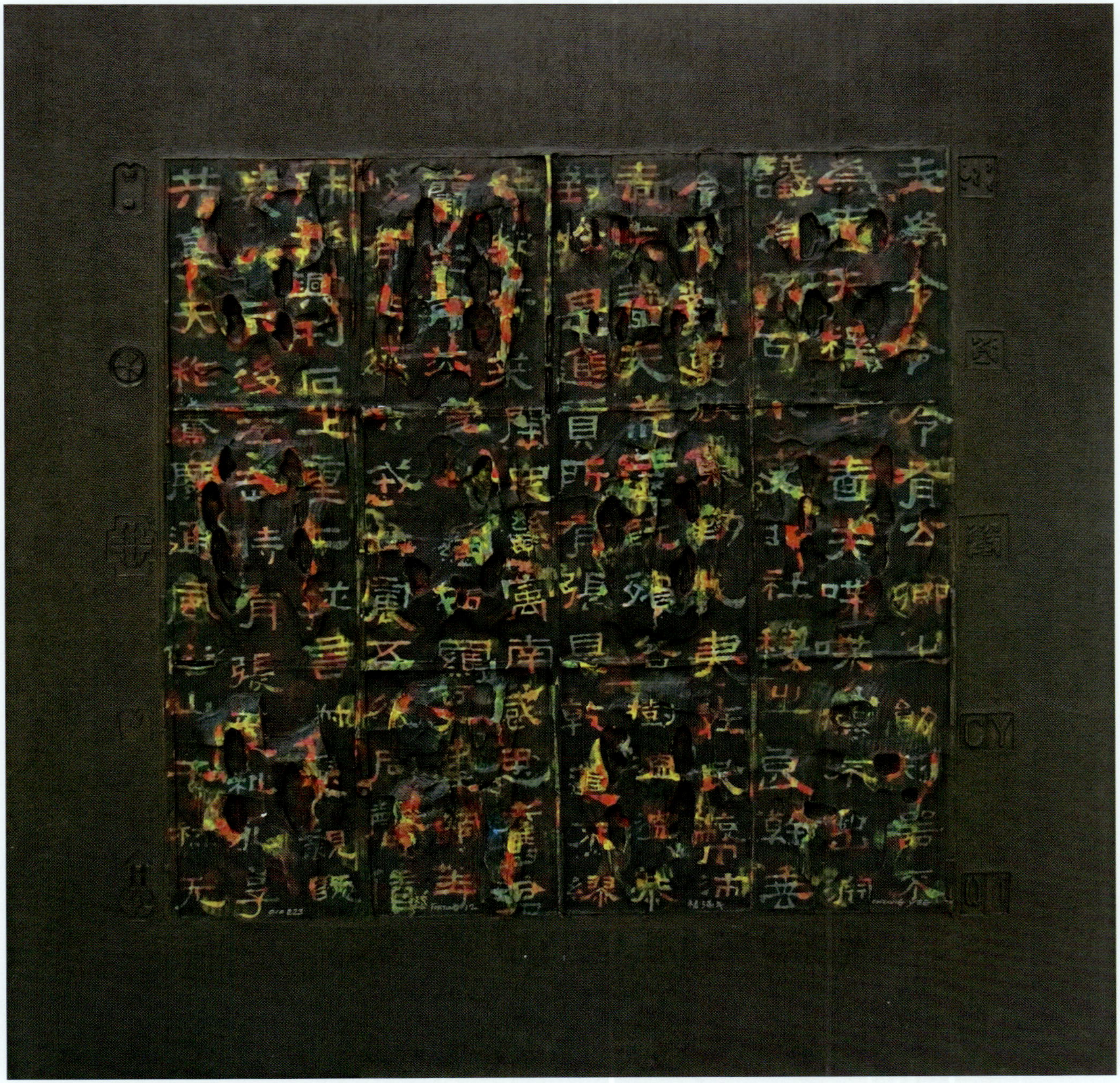

010223 FORTUNE 12
福滿年
Cast Paper on Wood
76.5 x 76.5 cm
2001

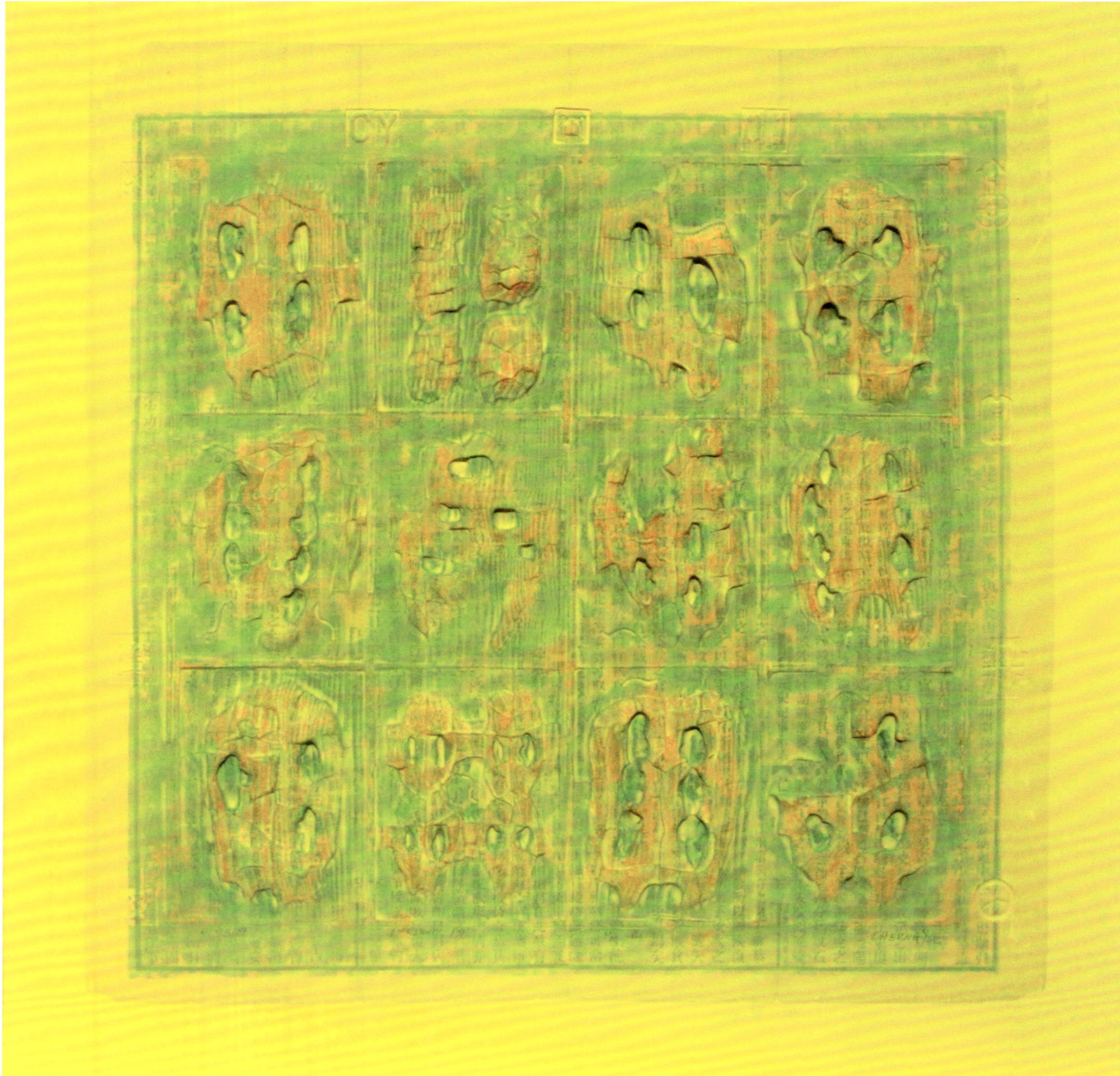

010318 FORTUNE 12
福滿年
Cast Paper on Wood
77 x 77 cm
2001

020319 MING
明
Cast Paper on Wood
76 x 76 cm
2002

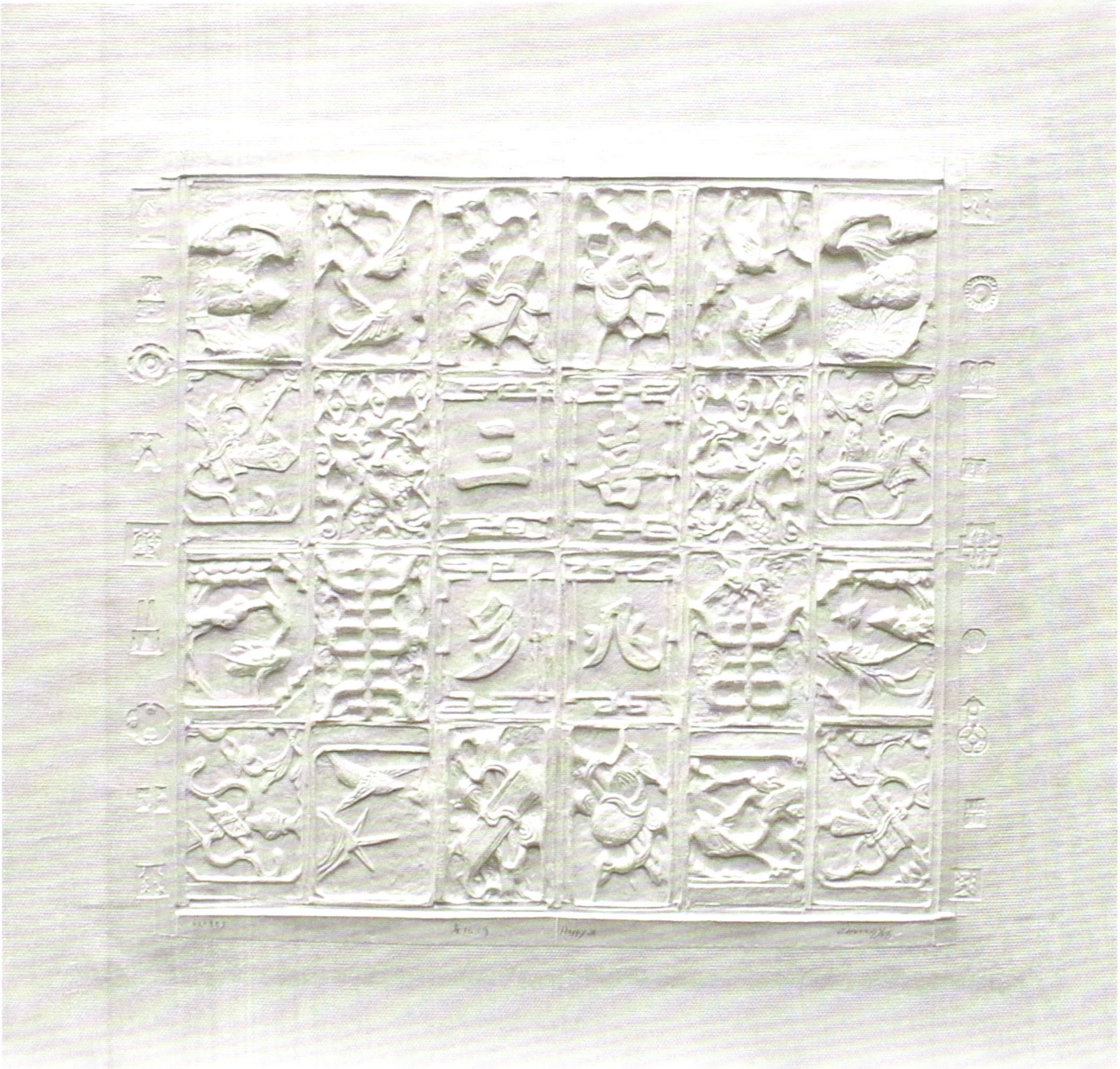

020323 Happy Three
喜兆三多
Cast Paper on Wood
92 x 91 cm
2002

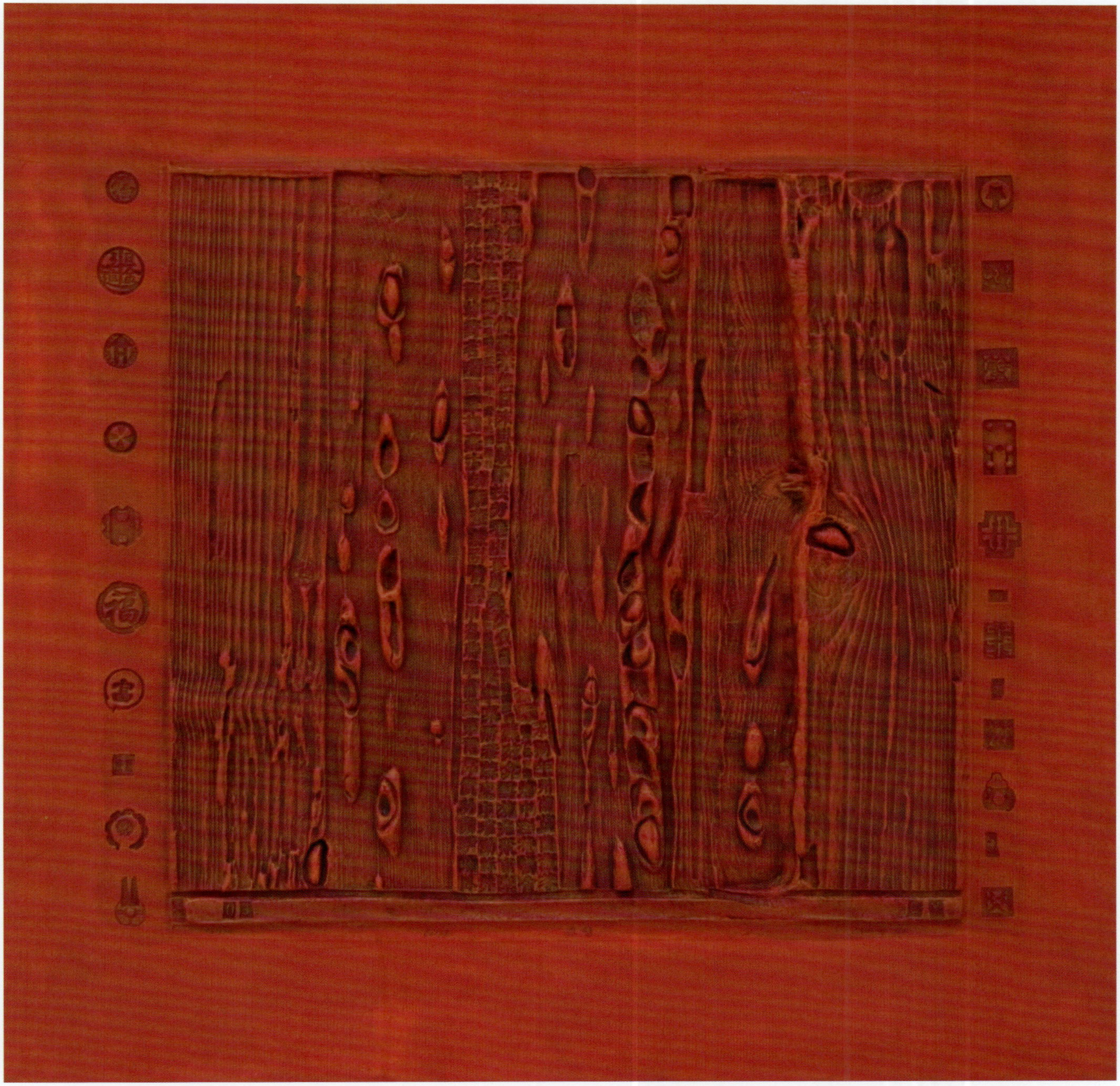

031202 CLIFF
赤壁
Cast Paper on Wood
92 x 92 cm
2003

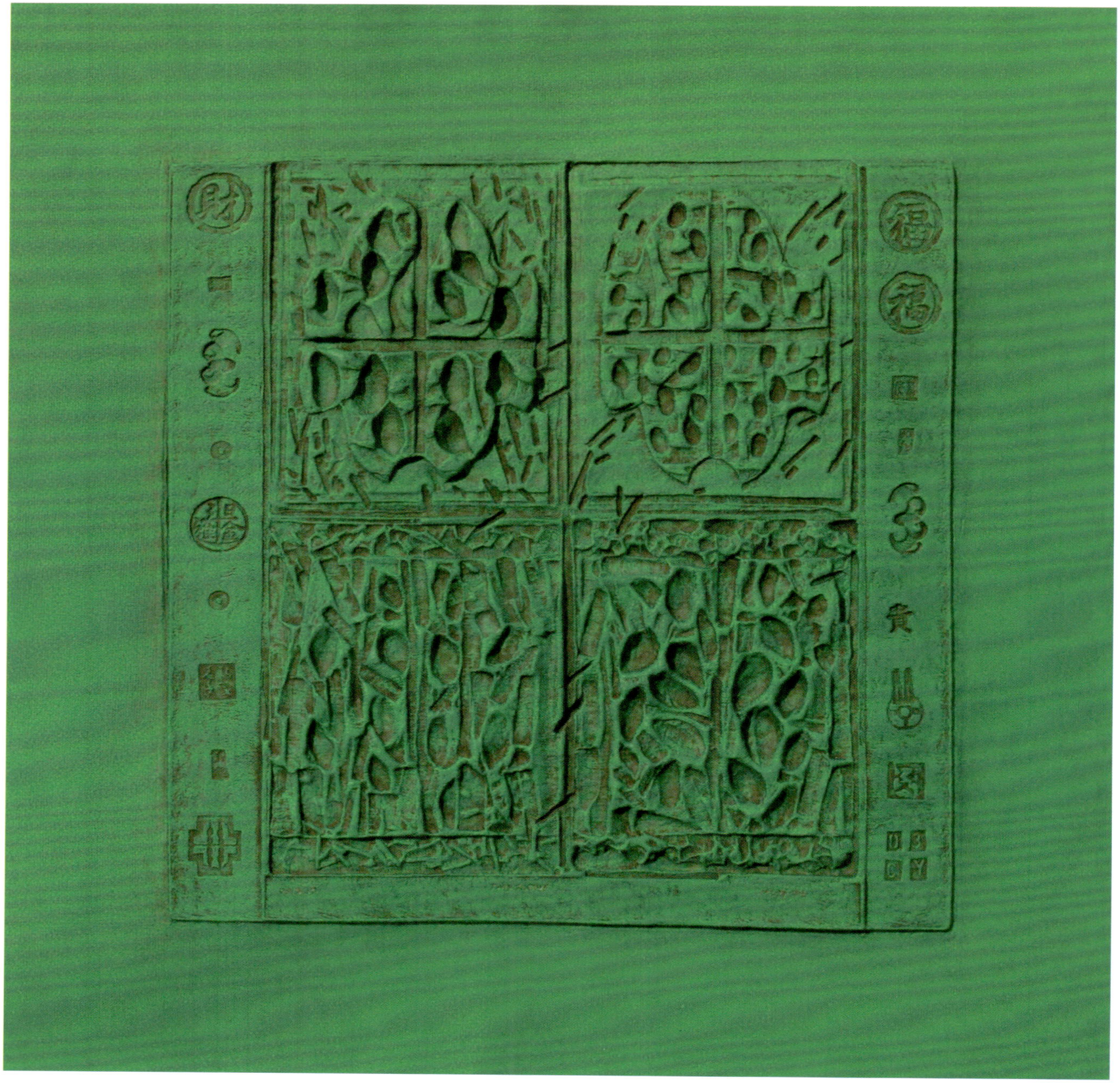

031228 Twin Fortune
雙福
Cast Paper on Wood
77 x 77 cm
2003

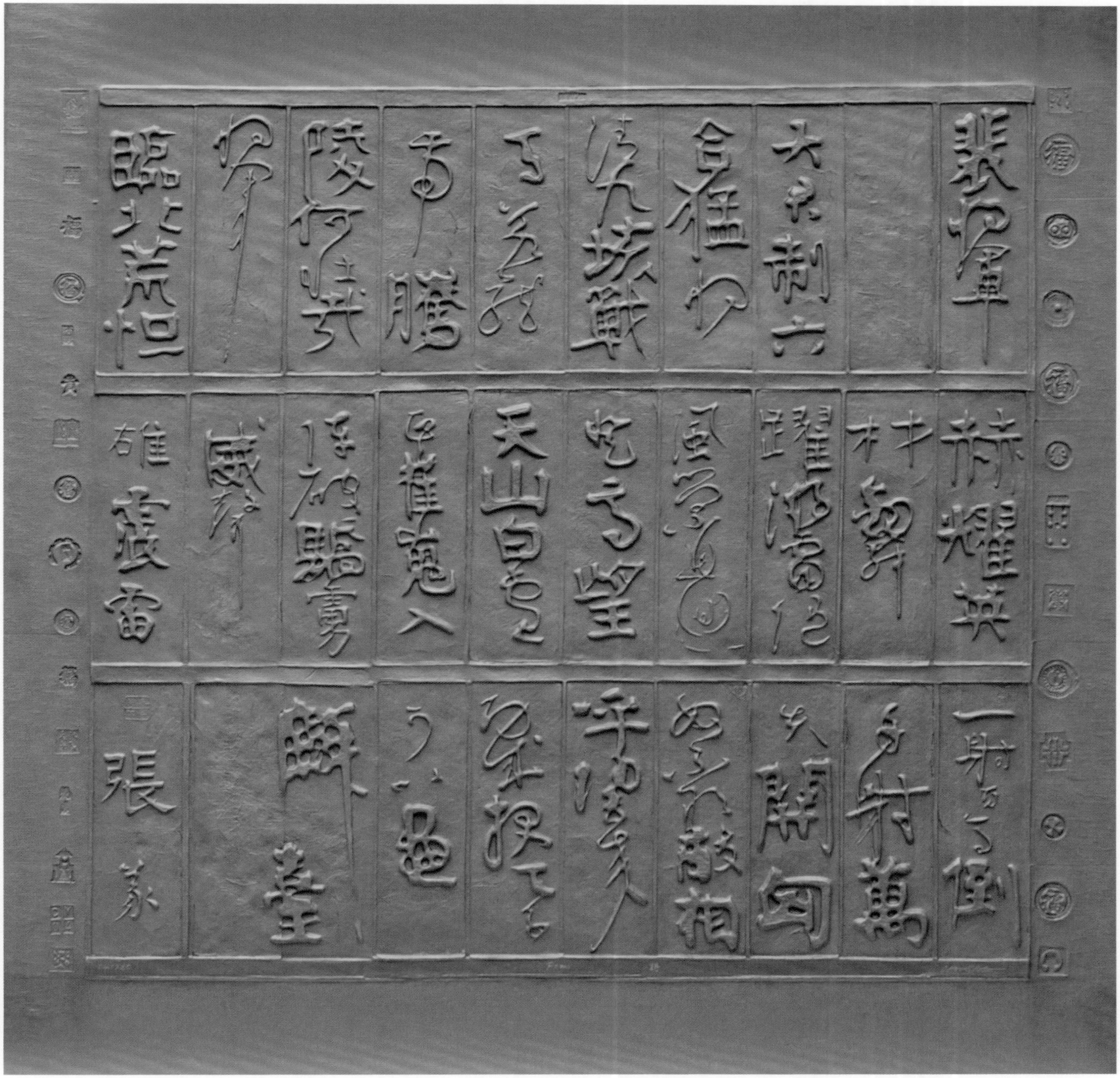

040320 POEM
詩
Cast Paper on Wood
122 x 122 cm
2004

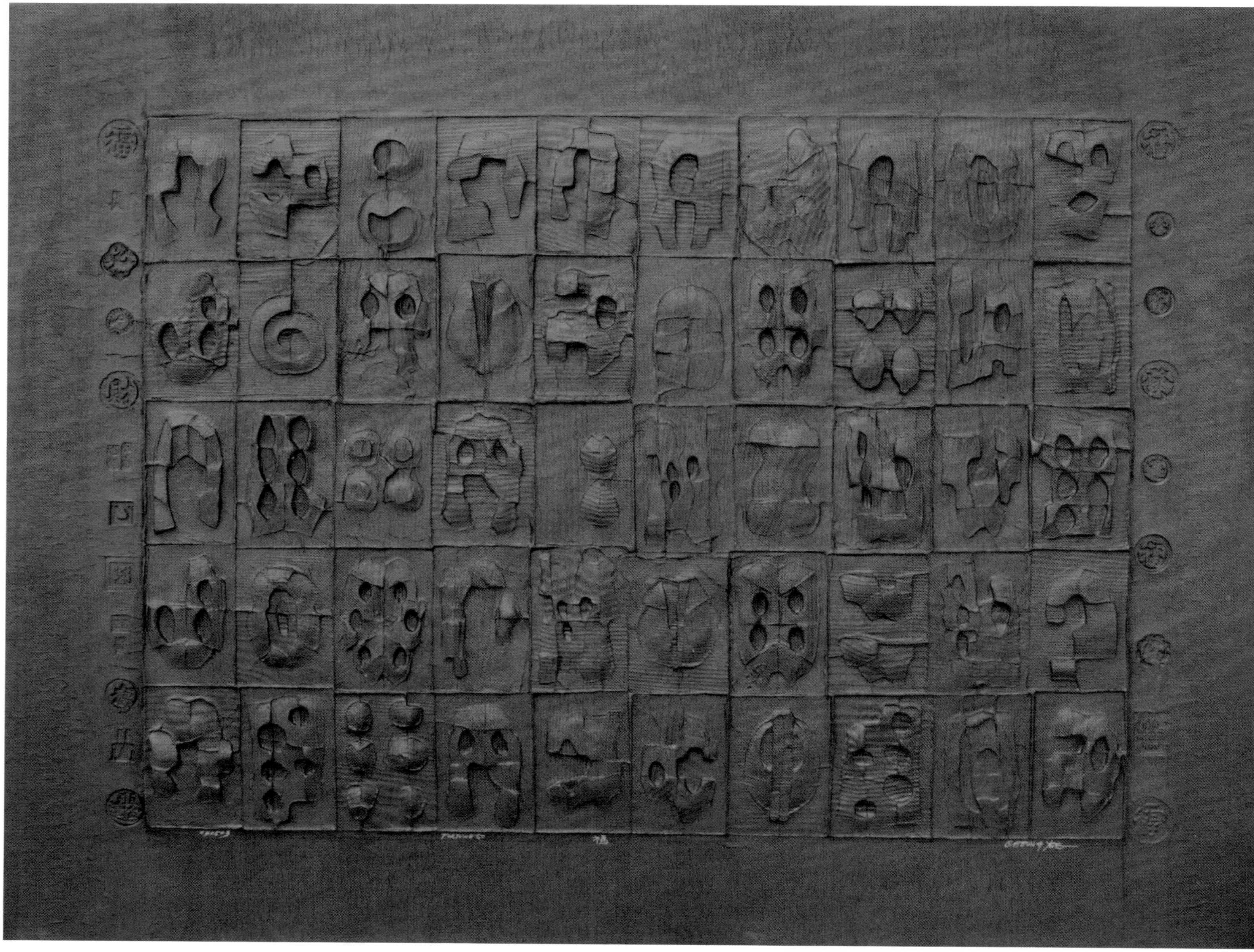

FORTUNE 50 040503
福
Cast Paper on Wood
101 x 132 cm
2004

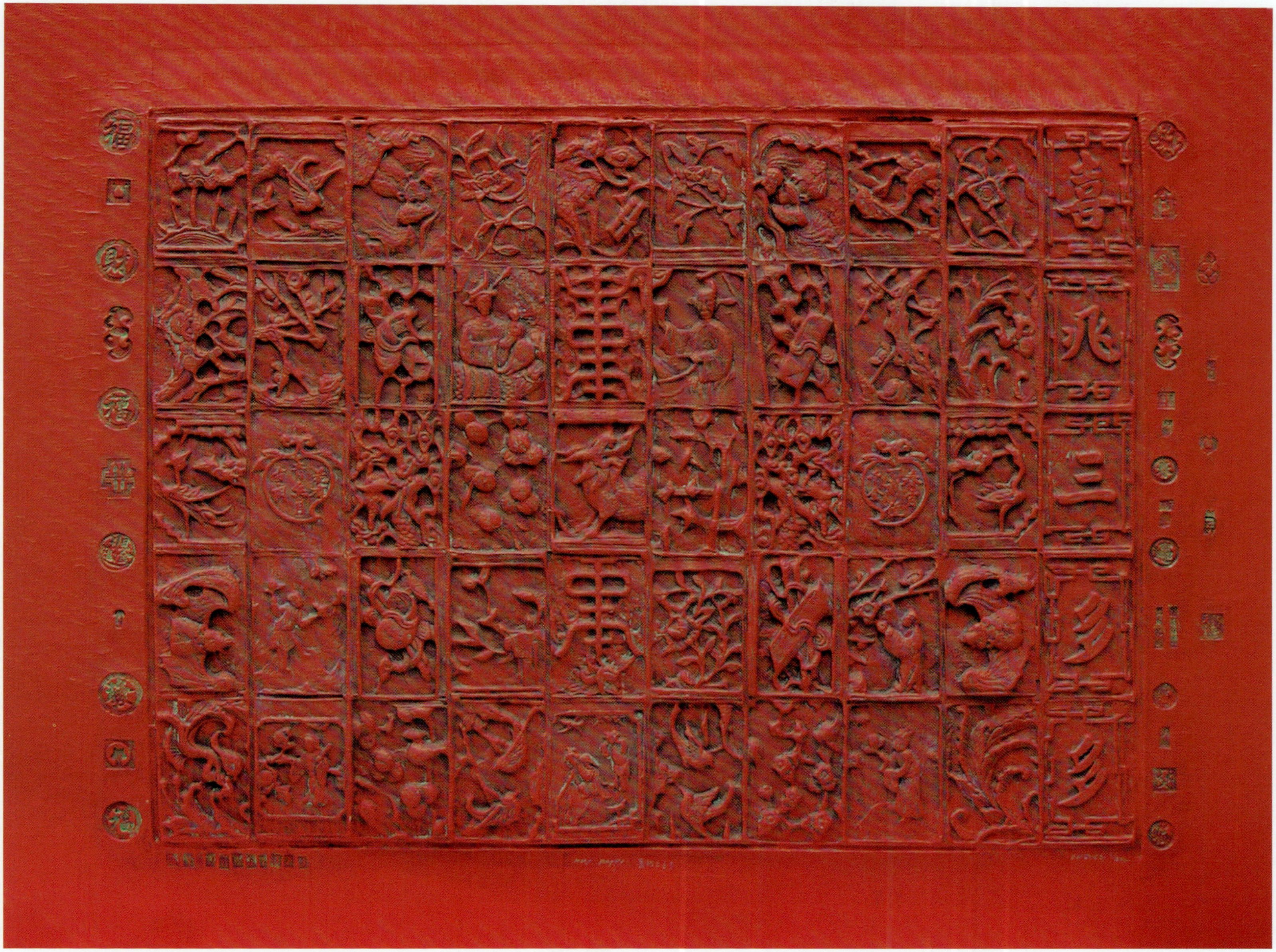

MORE HAPPY 041129
喜兆三多多
Cast Paper on Wood
100 x 130 cm
2004

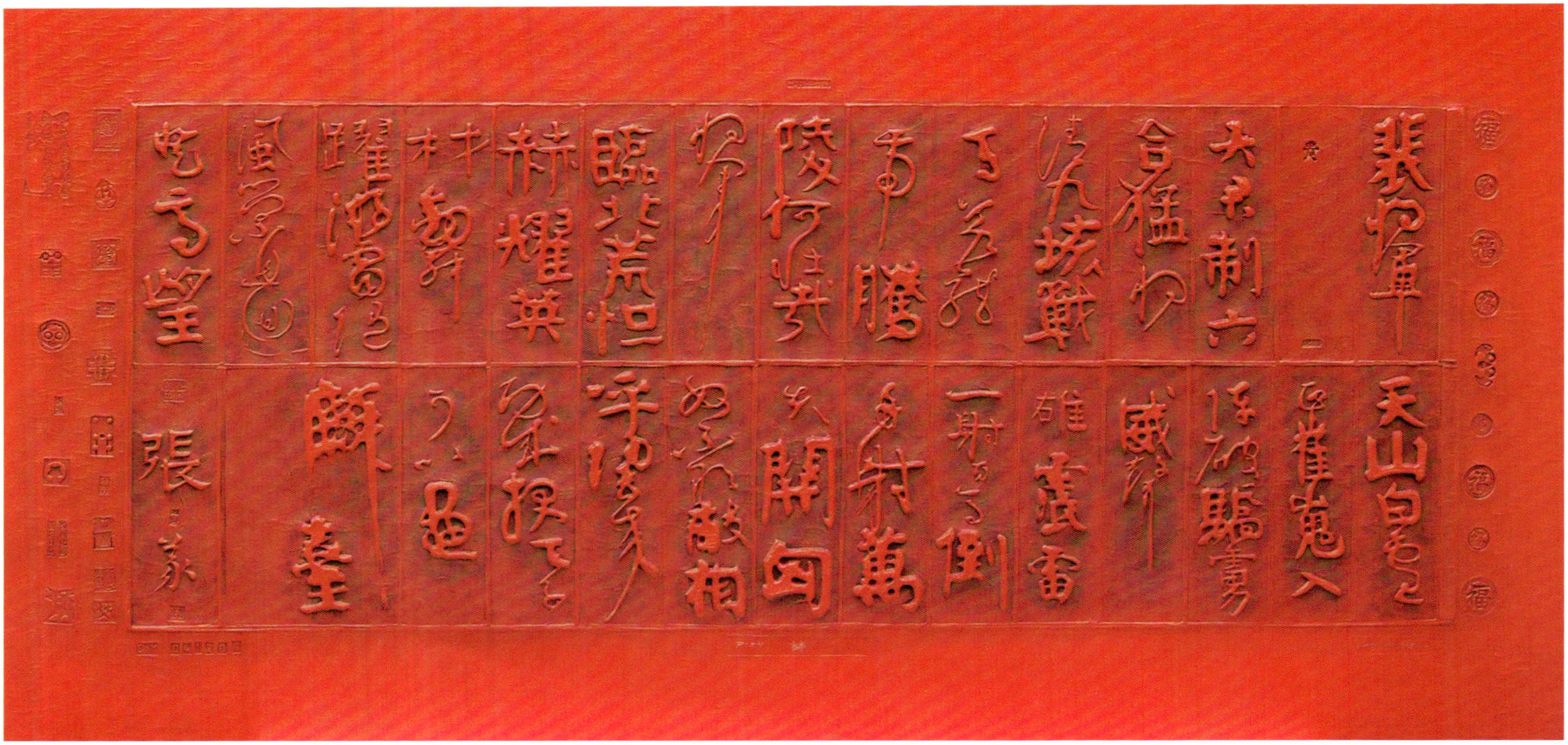

POEM 041208
詩
Cast Paper on Wood
92 x 183 cm
2005

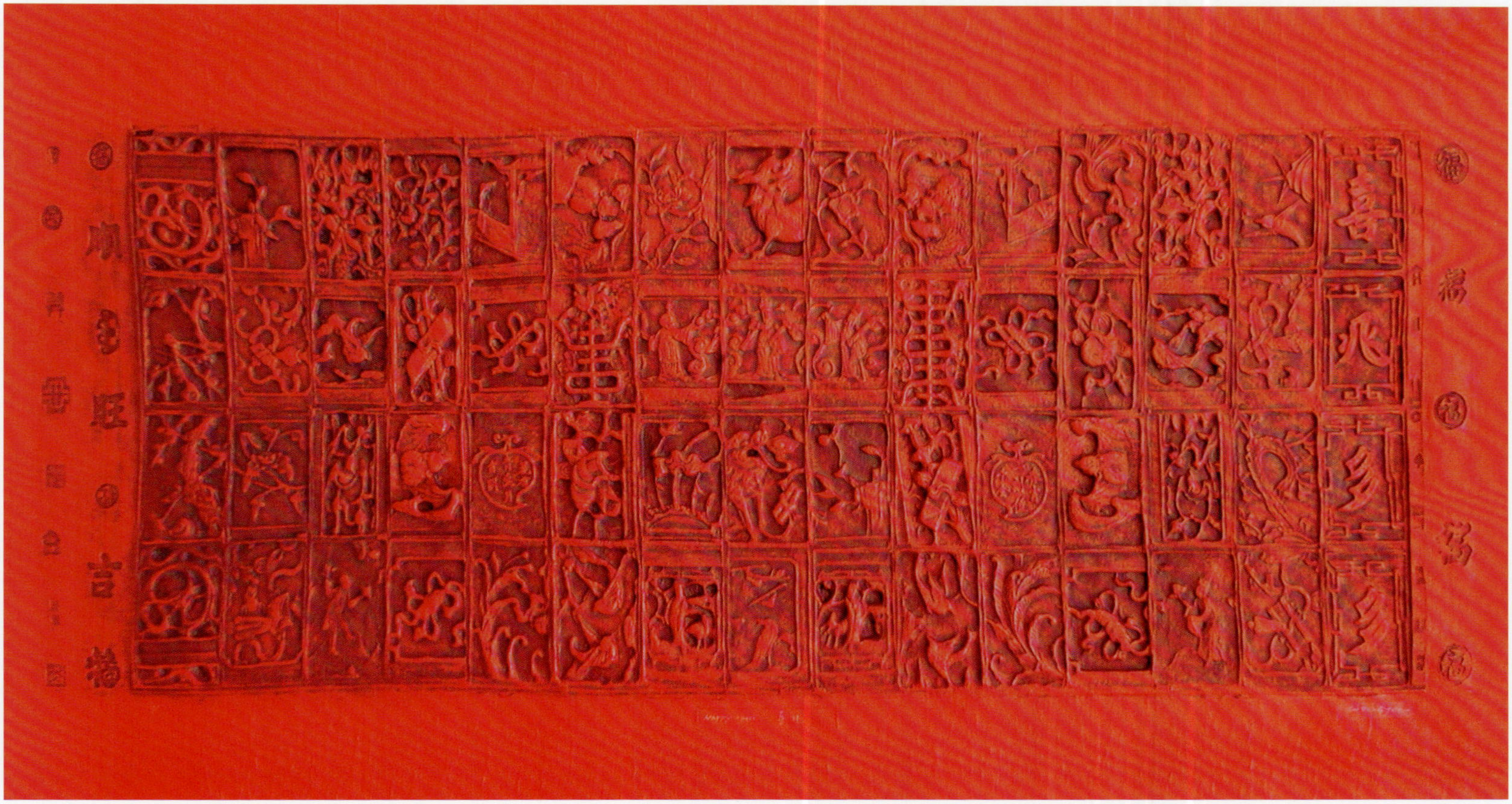

HAPPY THREE 50212
喜兆
Cast Paper on Wood
91.5 x 183.5 cm
2005

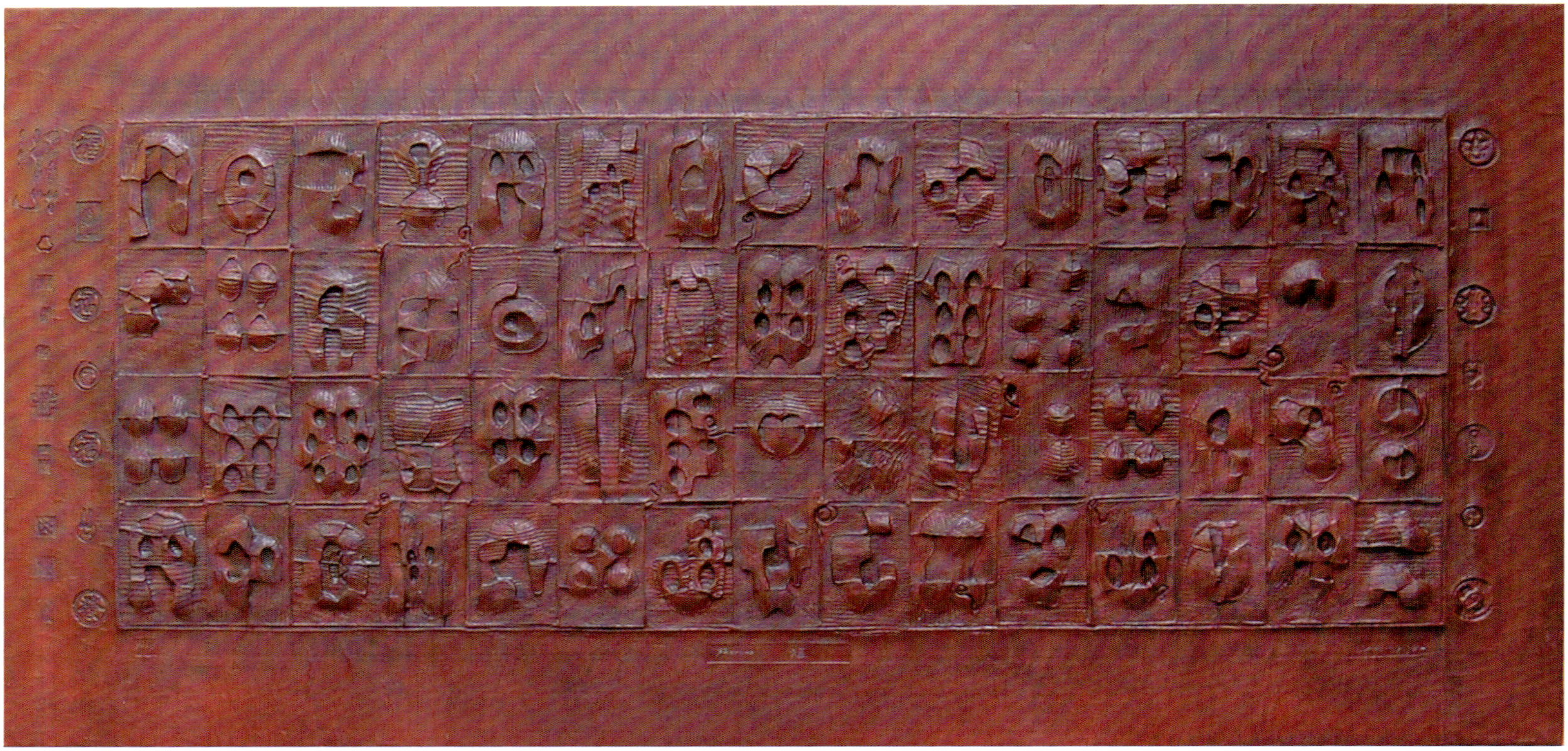

FORTUNE 50213
富
Cast Paper on Wood
91.5 x 183 cm
2005

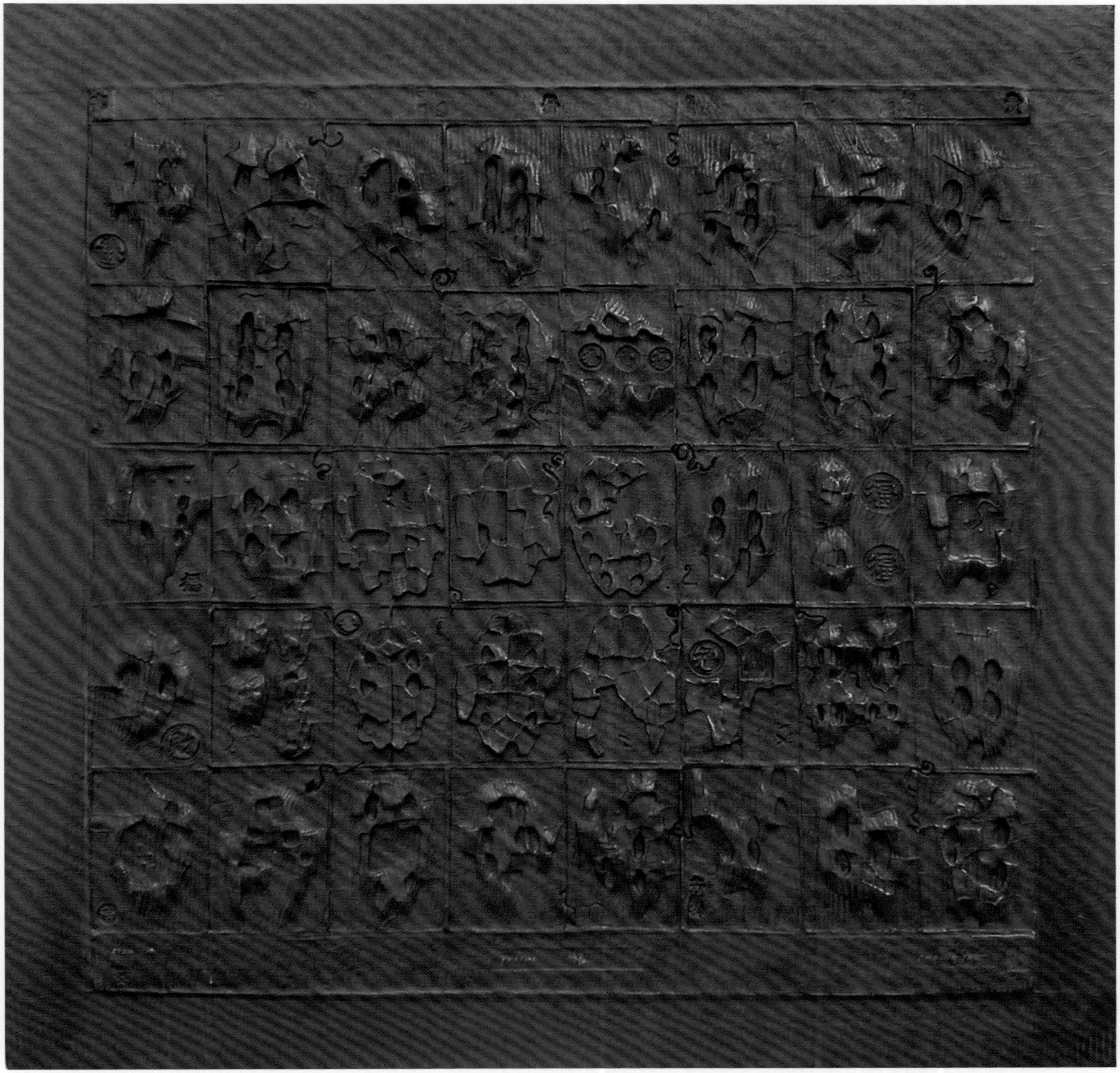

FORTUNE 50220
富
Cast Paper on Wood
122.5 x 122 cm
2005

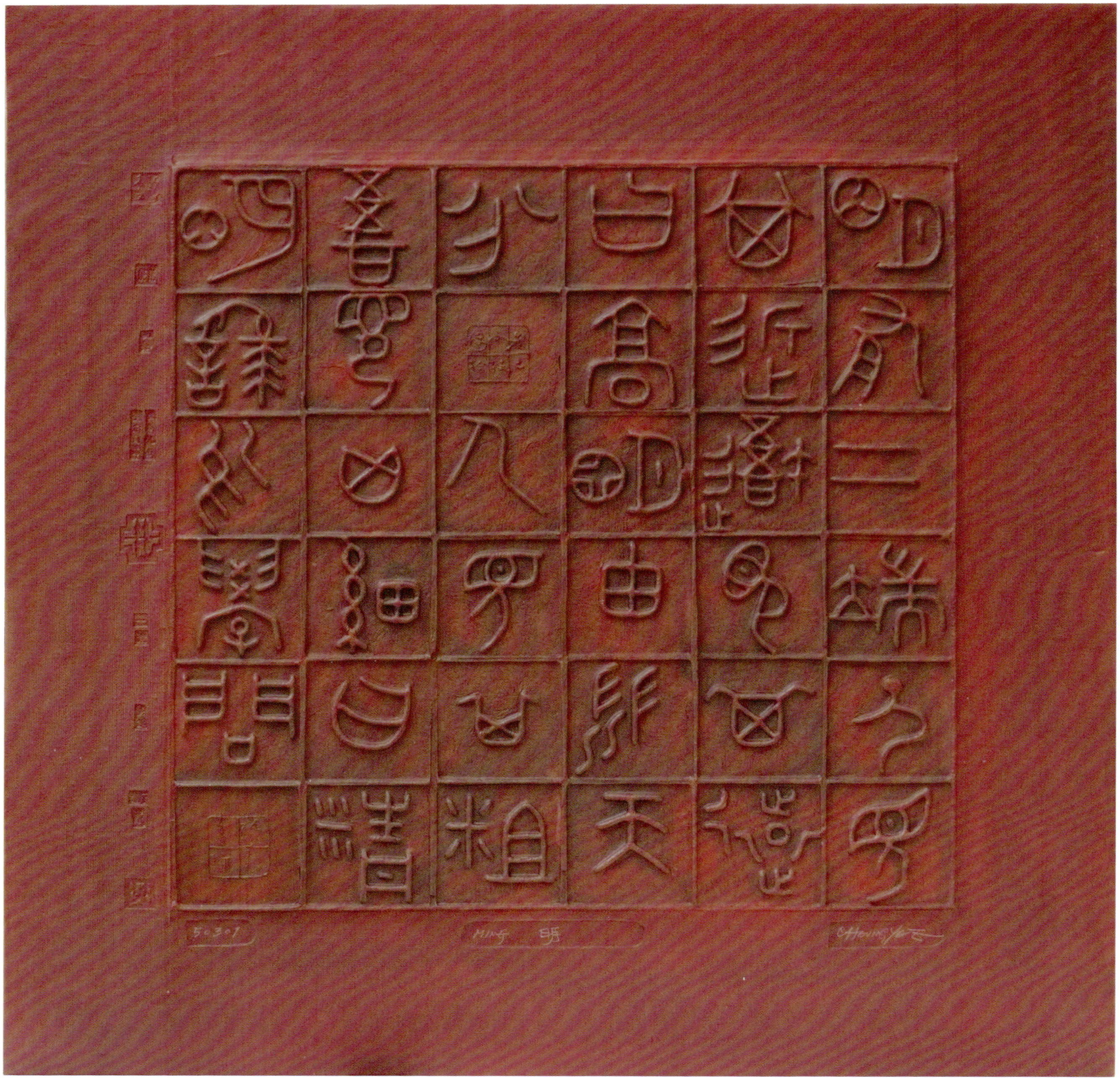

MING 50301
明
Cast Paper on Wood
92 x 92 cm
2005

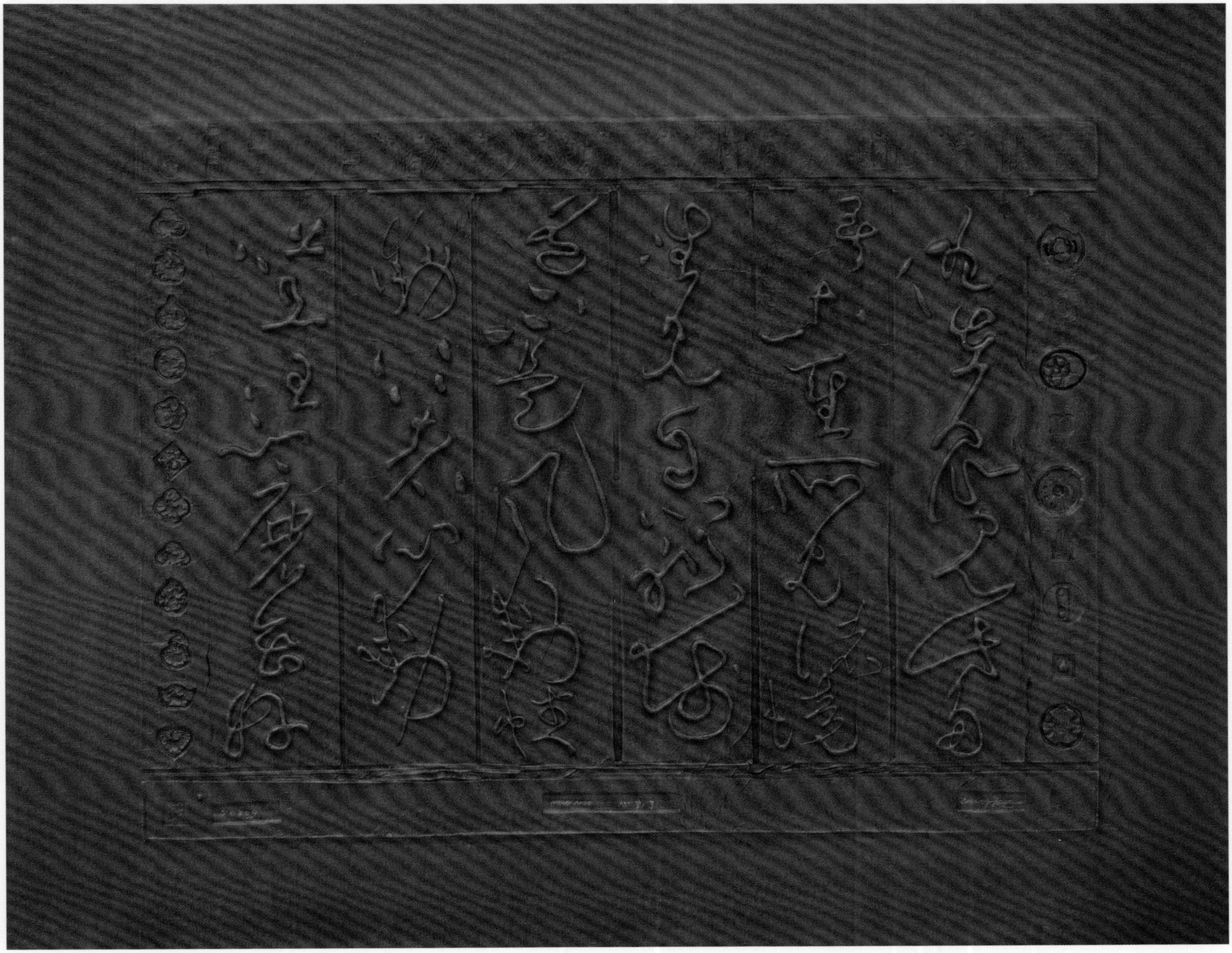

HEART MOVE 50309
心動了
Cast Paper on Wood
102 x 133 cm
2005

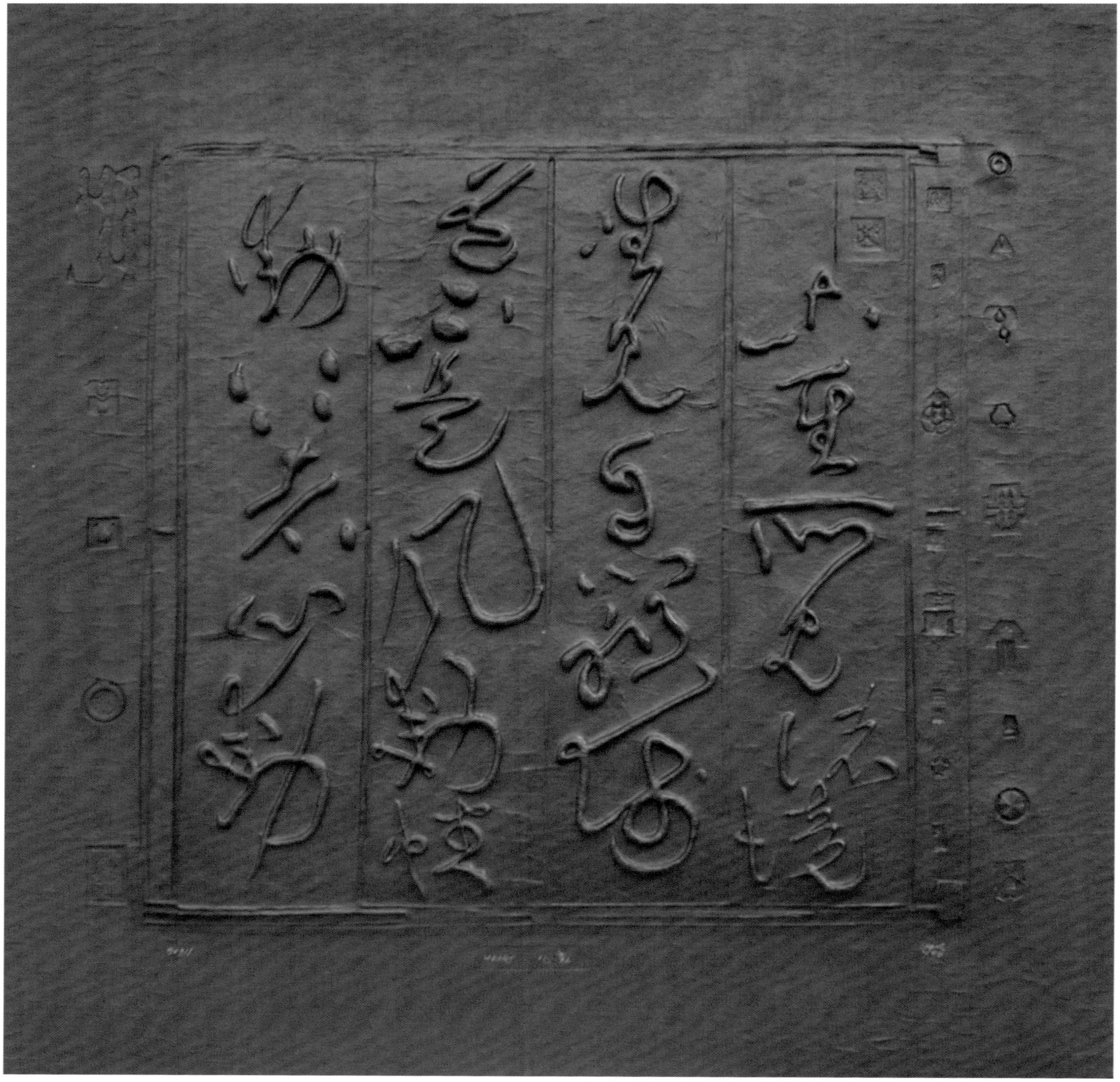

HEART 50311
心動
Cast Paper on Wood
91.5 x 91.5 cm
2005

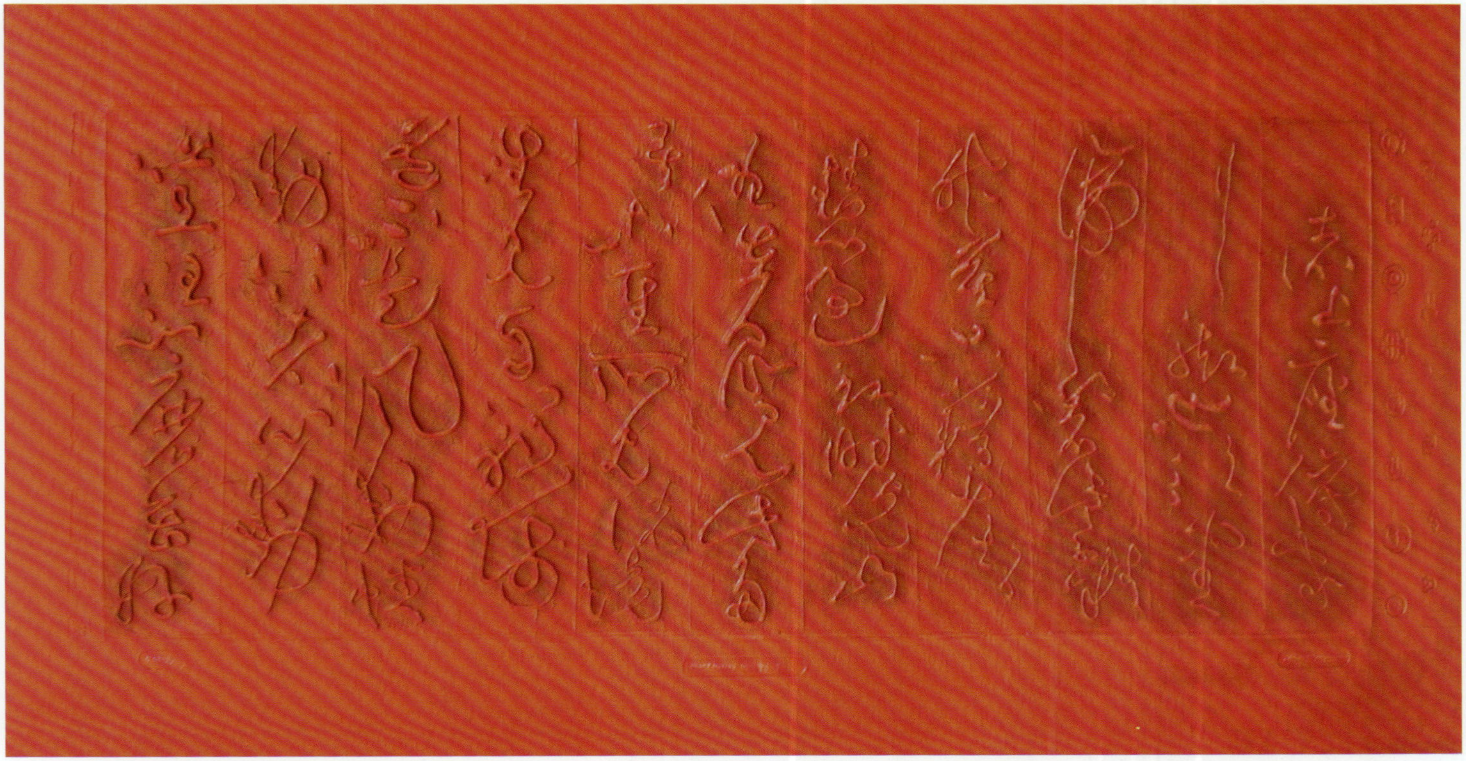

50803 Heart Moving
心動了
Cast Paper on Wood
92 x 183 cm
2005

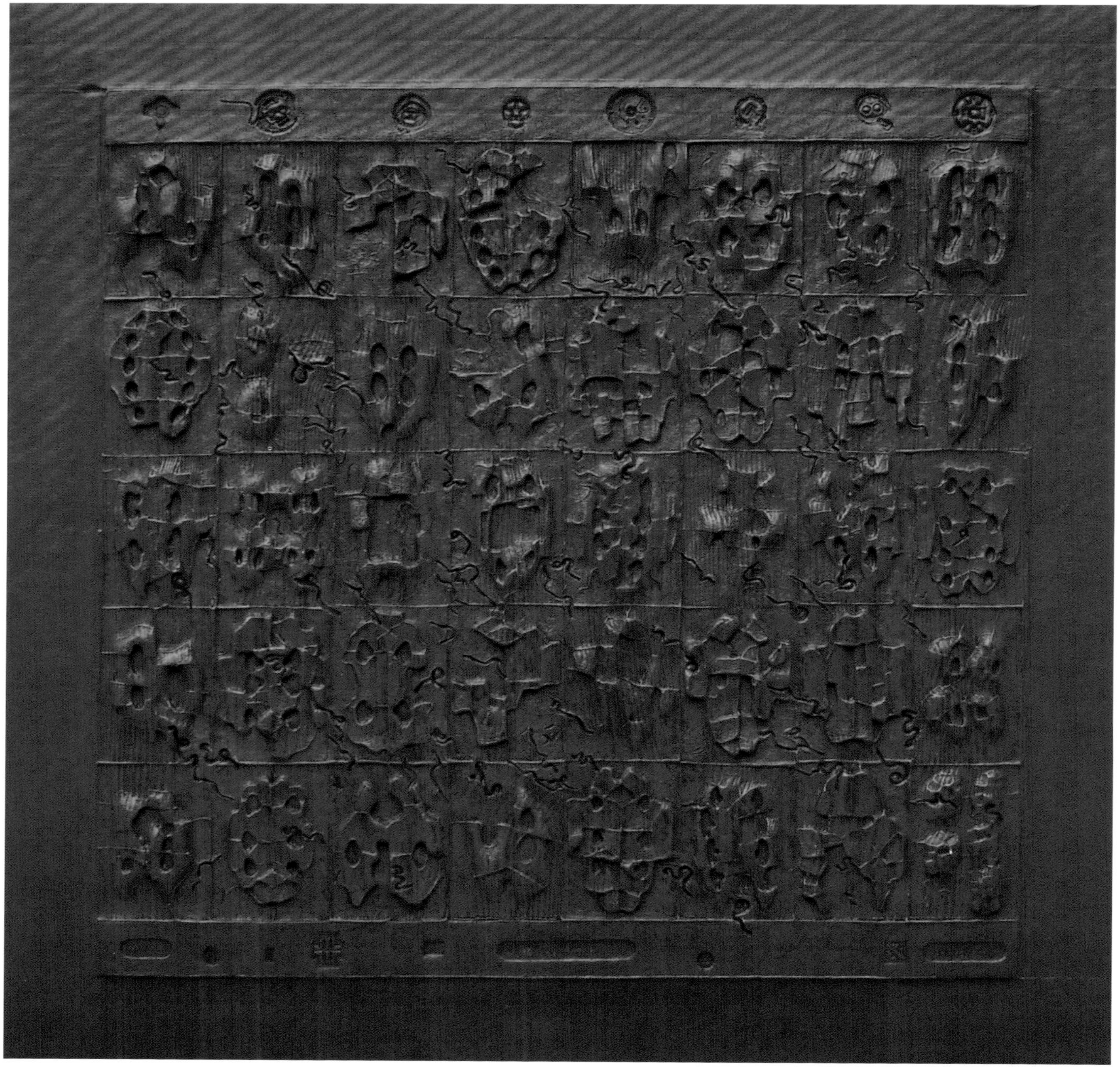

BIG FORTUNE 070101
大福
Cast Paper on Wood
121 x 122.5 cm
2007

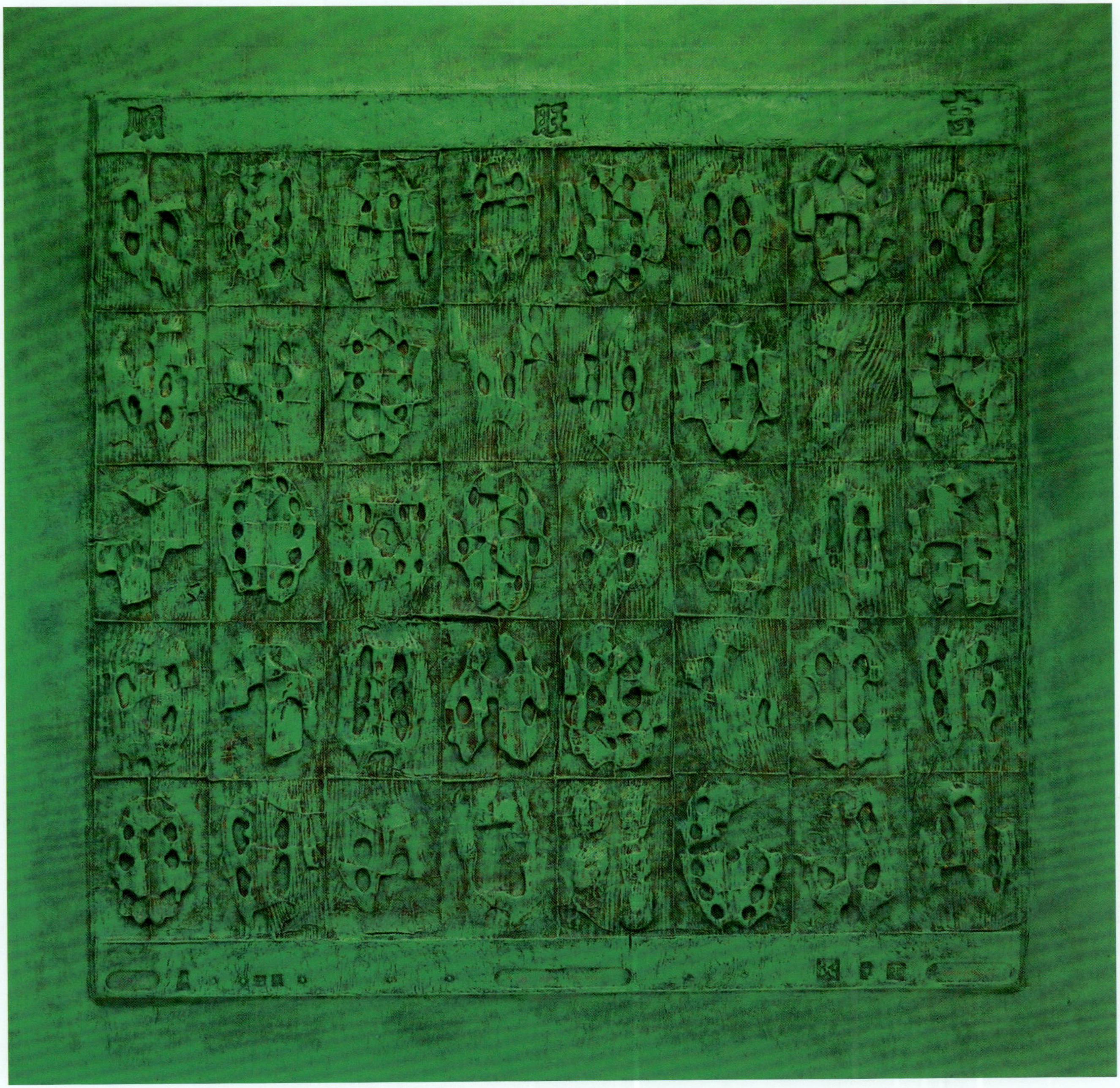

BIG FORTUNE 070102
大福
Cast Paper on Wood
122 x 122 cm
2007

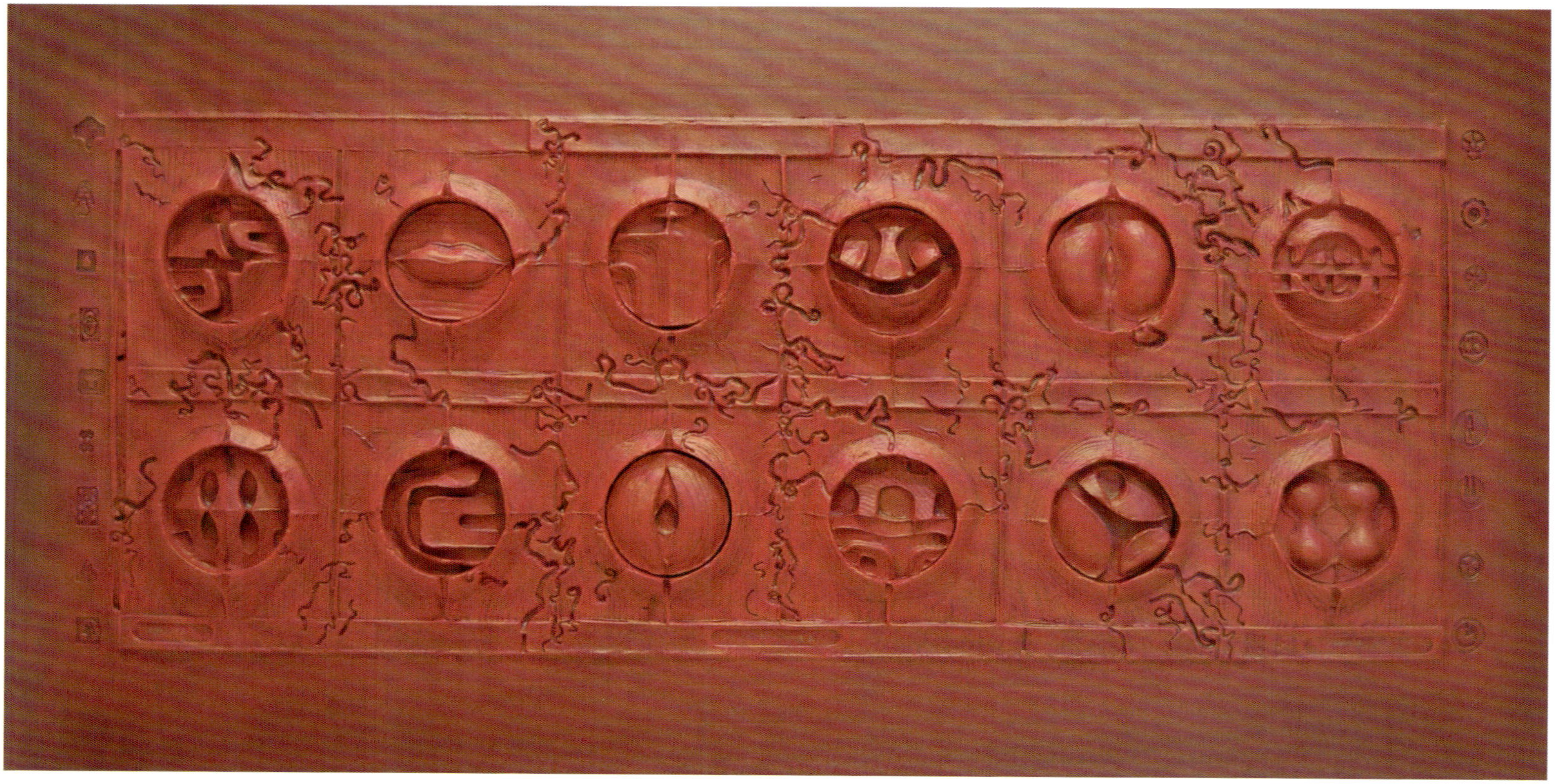

12 CIRCLES 070303
十二圓
Cast Paper on Wood
91.4 x 182.9 cm
2007

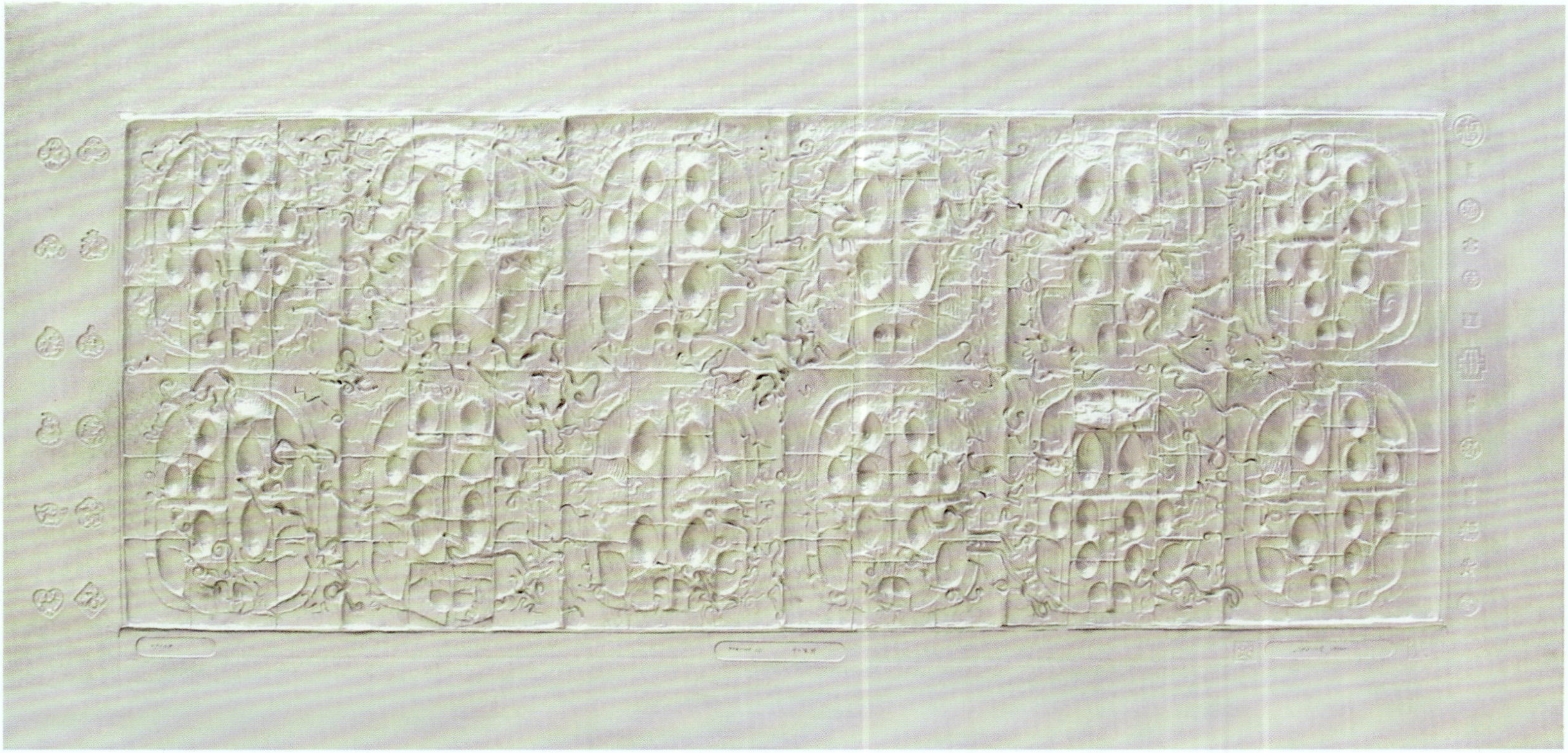

FORTUNE 12 073219
十二生肖
Cast Paper on Wood
92 x 183 cm
2007

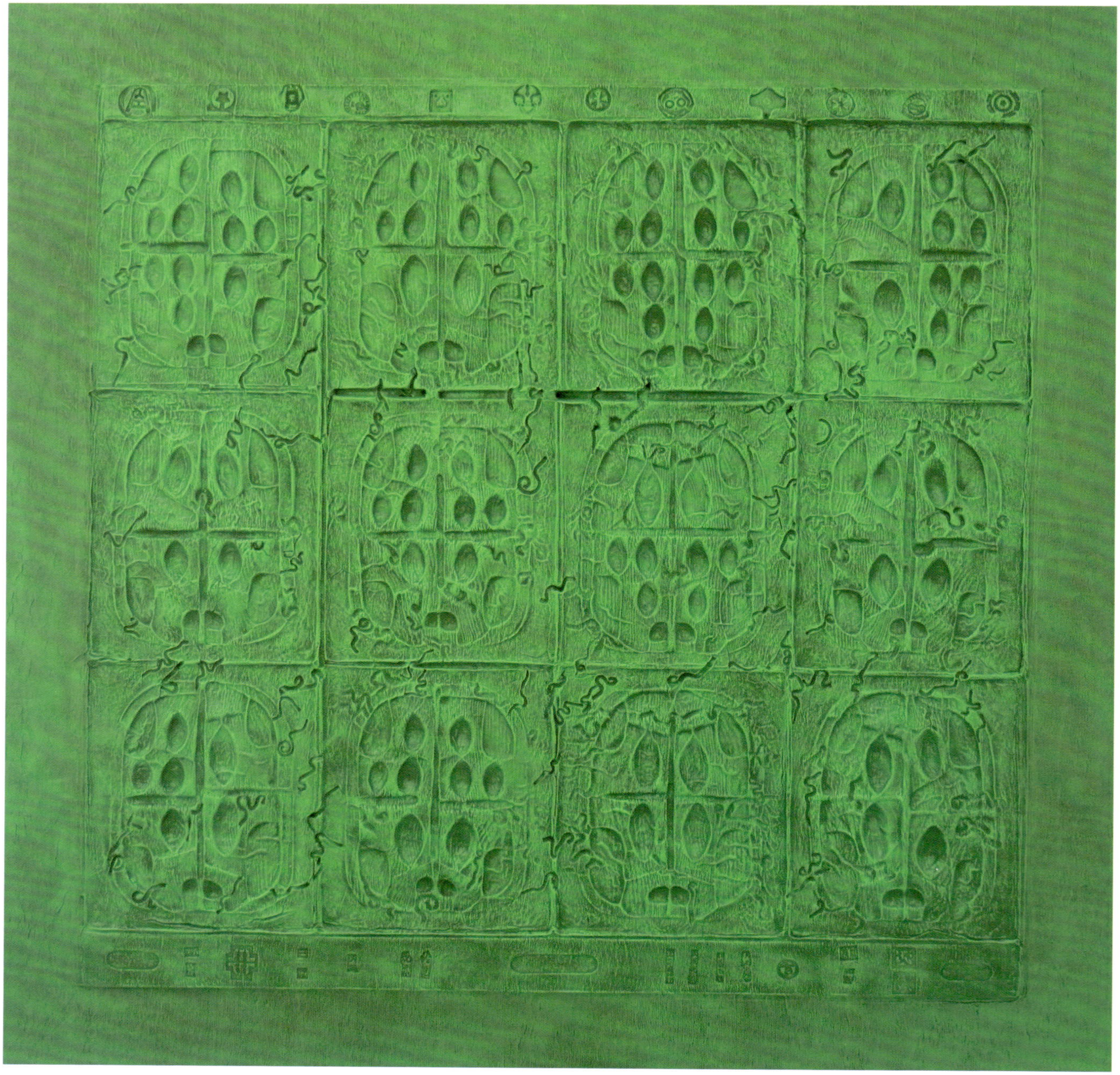

FORTUNE 12 070322
大福十二
Cast Paper on Wood
122 x 122 cm
2007

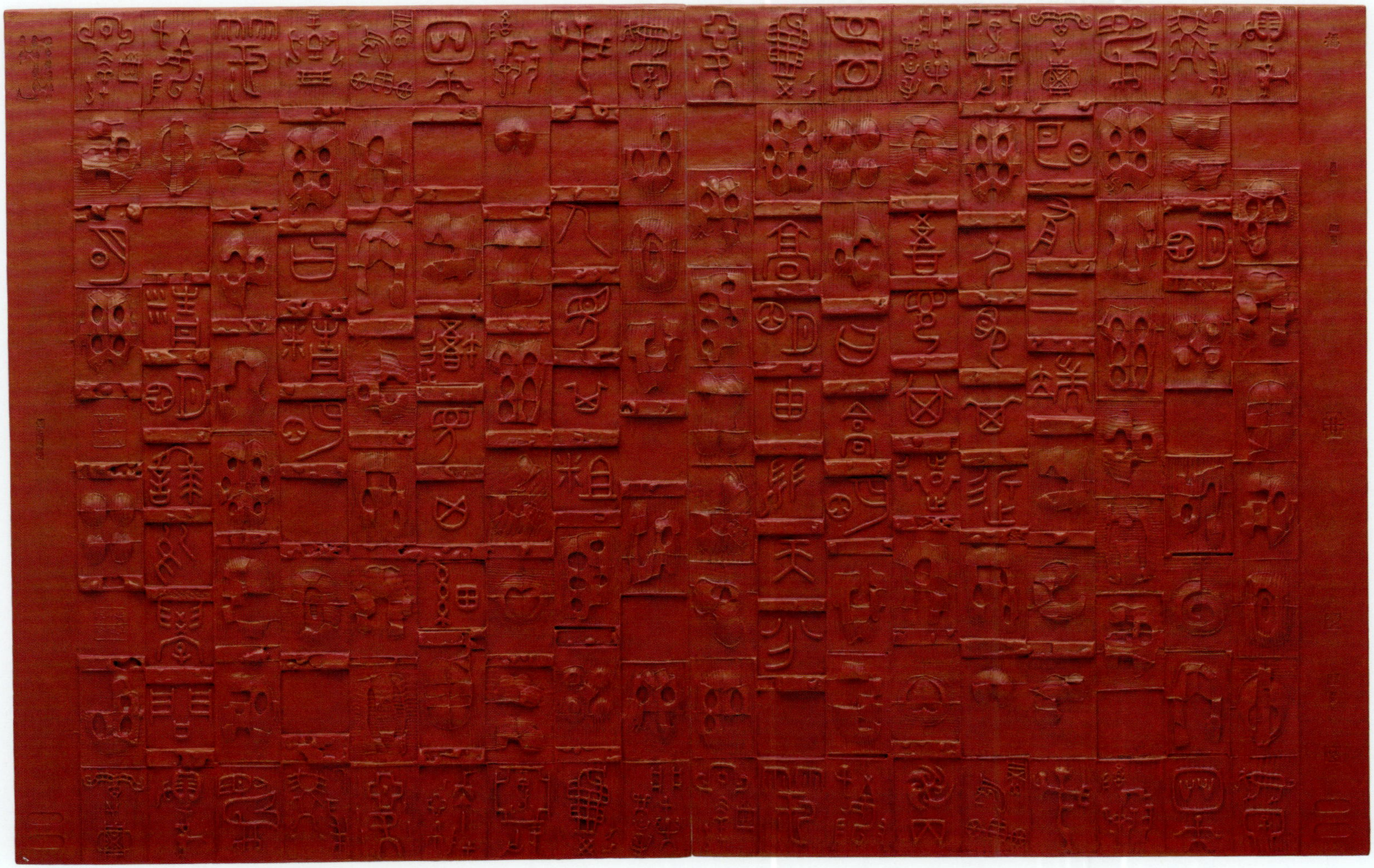

MING 070707
明
Cast Paper on Wood
132 x 203 cm (Diptych)
2007

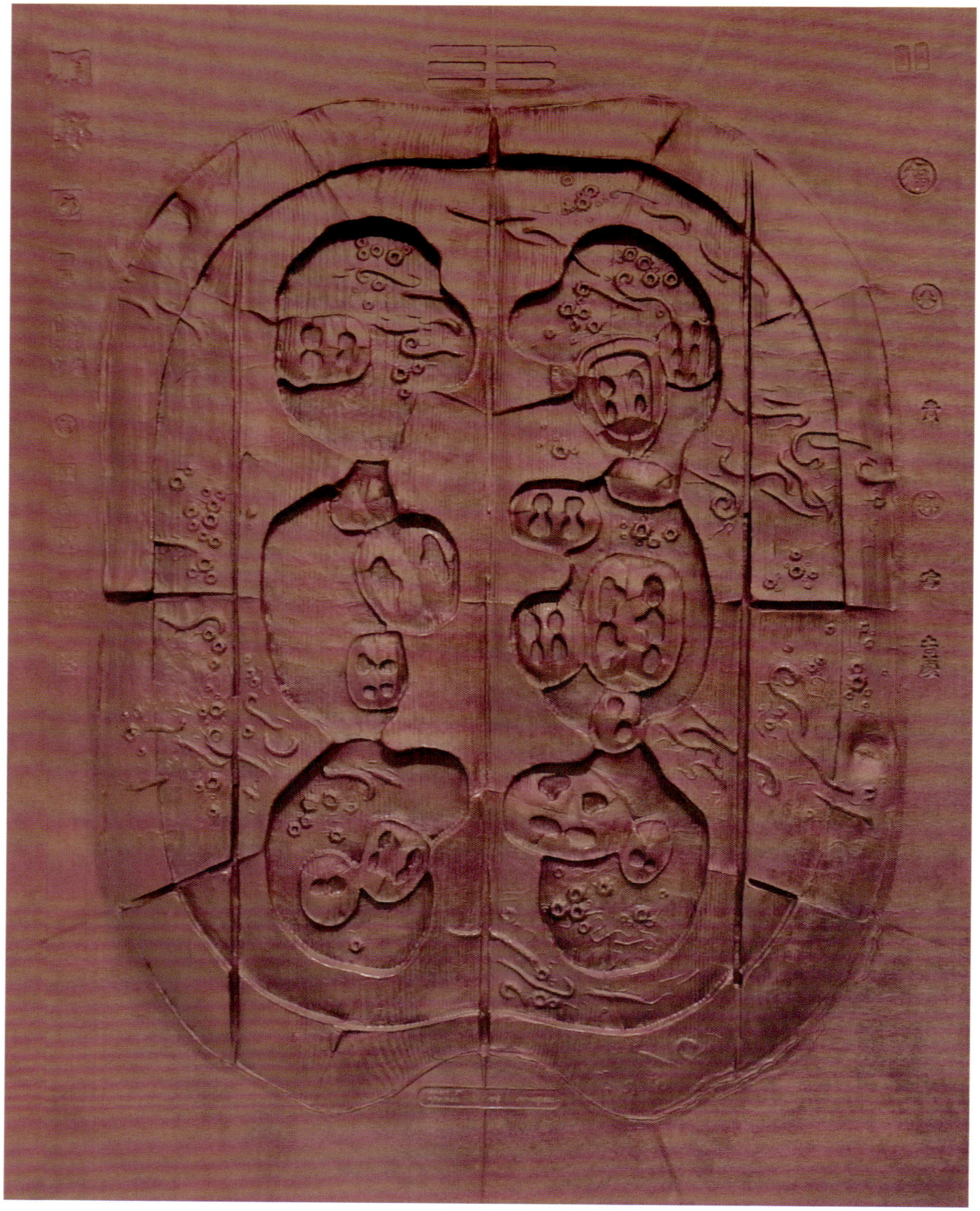

SPIRIT F 070323
坤
Cast Paper on Wood
132 x 102 cm
2007

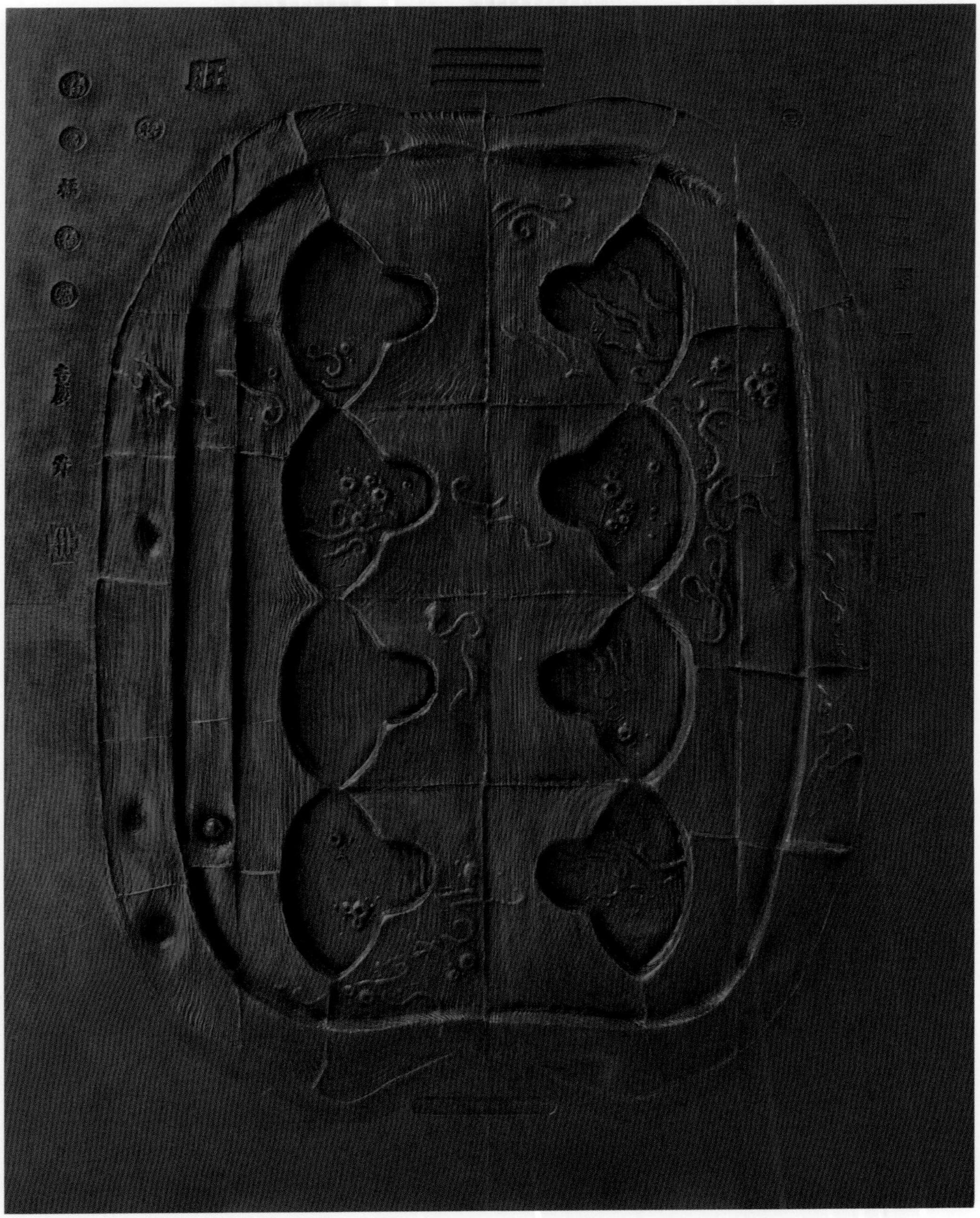

SPIRIT M 070328
乾
Cast Paper on Wood
132 x 102 cm
2007

CURRICULUM VITAE

簡歷

1936 Born in Guangzhou, China
1958 Graduated from the Fine Arts Department of National Taiwan Normal University
1963 Founded the Circle Group with other local artists
1965 Grant to U.S.A. and Europe from Institute of International Education
1968 - 73 Tutor in Extramural Studies Department, Chinese University of Hong Kong and University of Hong Kong
1976 Part Time lecturer, Department of Fine Arts, the Chinese University of Hong Kong
1978 - 83 Senior lecturer, Department of Design, Hong Kong Polytechnic
1979 Awarded the Member Order of the British Empire (Honorary)
1983 Lecturer, Department of Fine Arts, The Chinese University of Hong Kong
1984 - 92 Chairman, Department of Fine Arts, The Chinese University of Hong Kong
1987 Founding member of the Hong Kong Artists` Guild
1988 Awarded "Sculptor of the Year Award 1988", Hong Kong Artists` Guild

HONORARY SERVICES

Chairman, Hong Kong Sculptor Association
Advisor, Visual Art Society, Hong Kong
Advisor, Hong Kong Institute of Visual Studies
Advisor, Hong Kong Graphics Society
Advisor, Hong Kong Museum of Art

SOLO EXHIBITIONS

1964 City Museum and Art Gallery, Hong Kong
1965 Commonwealth Institute, London
1966 Sally Jackson Gallery, Hong Kong
1967 The Luz Gallery, Manila
1969 U.S.I.S. Library, Hong Kong
University of Hong Kong
Thor Gallery, Louisville, KY, U.S.A.
The Luz Gallery, Manila
1974 The Luz Gallery, Manila
1976 Hong Kong Arts Centre
1978 Hong Kong Museum of Art
Pacific Gallery, San Francisco, U.S.A.
1979 Printmakers Art Gallery, Taiwan
1985 Hsiung Shih Gallery, Taipei, Taiwan
1987 Yuen Long Town Hall, Hong Kong
1988 Hsiung Shih Gallery, Taipei, Taiwan
Galerie Du Monde, Hong Kong
1992 Hsiung Shih Gallery, Taipei, Taiwan
1993 Hong Kong Museum of Art
1994 Artpreciation Gallery, Hong Kong
1996 Artpreciation Gallery, Hong Kong
1999 Alliance Francaise de Singapour

1936 生於中國廣州
1958 畢業於臺灣國立師範大學藝術系
1963 與本港藝術家創立中元畫會
1965 獲紐約國際教育學院頒贈獎學金，赴美及歐洲進修
1968 － 73 任教香港大學及中文大學校外課程部
1976 任教香港中文大學藝術系，為兼任講師
1978 － 83 任香港理工學院太古設計學院高級講師
1979 獲英國政府頒贈榮譽MBE勳銜
1983 任教香港中文大學藝術系
1984 － 92 香港中文大學藝術系系主任
1987 香港藝術家聯盟創會會員
1988 香港藝術家聯盟頒贈“香港1988雕刻家年獎”

顧問

香港雕塑家協會主席
視覺藝術協會顧問
香港正形設計研究院顧問
香港版畫協會顧問
香港藝術館榮譽顧問

個人展覽

1964 香港博物美術館
1965 倫敦英聯邦學院
1966 香港三集畫廊
1967 菲律賓馬尼拉盧茨畫廊
1969 香港美國圖書館
香港大學
美國肯塔基州霍柯畫廊
菲律賓馬尼拉盧茨畫廊
1974 菲律賓馬尼拉盧茨畫廊
1976 香港藝術中心
1978 香港藝術館
美國三藩市太平洋畫廊
1979 台灣台北版畫家畫廊
1980 美國三藩市悟畫廊
1985 台灣台北雄獅畫廊
1987 香港新界元朗大會堂
1988 台灣台北雄獅畫廊
香港杜蒙畫廊
1992 台灣台北雄獅畫廊
1993 香港藝術館
1994 香港誰先覺
1996 香港誰先覺
1999 星加坡法國文化協會

2000 Nanyang Academy of Fine Art, Singapore
Alliance Francaise de Singapour
DP Space, Singapore
2002 iPreciation, Singapore
2003 iPreciation, Singapore
2005 iPreciation in collaboration with Jeff Hsu's Art, Taiwan
2008 iPreciation, Singapore

COLLECTIONS

Hong Kong Museum of Art, Hong Kong
Hong Kong Heritage Museum, Hong Kong
Ashmolen Museum, Oxford, England
Museum of Modern Art, Mexico City
National Museum of History, Taipei, Taiwan
Taipei Fine Arts Museum, Taiwan
Taiwan Museum of Art, Tai Chung, Taiwan
Kaohsiung Museum of Fine Arts, Taiwan

Private collections in Sweden, Switzerland, England, Germany, Italy, Spain, France, Greece, U.S.A., Canada, Mexico, Brazil, Australia, New Zealand, Japan, Hong Kong, Taiwan, India, Thailand, Philippines, Sri Lanka, Malaysia and Singapore.

GROUP EXHIBITIONS

1960 Pittori Cinesi Contemporanie, Roma
1961 Salon d`Aout, Hong Kong, St. John Cathedral Hall
1962 Hong Kong Art Today, City Museum and Art Gallery, Hong Kong
2nd International Salon of Arts, Hong Kong (also in `63)
Hong Kong Artists, Chatham Galleries, Hong Kong
1st International Art Exhibition in Saigon. (Awarded)
Joint Exhibition of Cheung Yee and Lam Chun-fai, City Hall, Hong Kong
1964 1st Circle Group Show, Hong Kong (Also in `65, `66, `67, `68, `69, `70)
Pittsburgh International, Carnegie Institute, U.S.A.
1965 Traveling Exhibition in South East Asia
Bayreuth International, Germany
1966 Hong Kong Artist, Sally Jackson Gallery
1967 Exhibition of City Museum and Art Gallery`s Collection, Hong Kong
1968 The Artist`s Eye of Hong Kong, City Museum and Art Gallery, Hong Kong
1969 Sculpture Model and Sketch Exhibition, City Museum and Art Gallery, Hong Kong
Exhibition of Contemporary Hong Kong Art, City Museum and Art Gallery, Hong Kong (also in `71,`72,`75,`77)
1970 Expo' 70, Hong Kong Pavilion, Japan
Four Artists of Hong Kong, City Museum and Art Gallery, Hong Kong
1971 Art Now Hong Kong, London, Edinburgh, Manchester, Bristol
2nd Triennale of Contemporary Art, New Delhi, India
1976 Critic's Choice, St. John's Ambulance Assn. Hong Kong
Art 76, Fung Ping Shan Museum, University of Hong Kong (also in `78,`81,`84)
1977 First Choice, St. John's Ambulance Assn. Hong Kong (also in `78,`79,`80,`82,`83,`84,`85,`86 at Hong Kong Arts Centre)
Inaugural Exhibition, Hong Kong Arts Centre
1979 Sketches By Three Hong Kong Artists, Hong Kong Arts Centre

2000 星加坡南洋藝術學院
星加坡法國文化協會
星加坡 DP 空間
2002 星加坡誰先覺
2003 星加坡誰先覺
2005 星加坡誰先覺及台灣觀想藝術合辦
2008 星加坡誰先覺

收藏
香港藝術館，香港
香港文化博物館，香港
阿什莫爾博物館，牛津，英國
墨西哥城現代美術館，墨西哥
台北國立歷史博物館，台灣
台北市立美術館，台灣
台灣省立美術館，台灣
高雄市立美術館，台灣

私人蒐集：香港，台灣，菲律賓，瑞典，瑞士，英國，美國，加拿大，日本，德國，澳洲，泰國，墨西哥，巴西，意大利，希臘，印度，斯里蘭卡，西班牙，法國，紐西蘭，馬來西亞，星加坡等地

主要聯展
1960 當代中國藝術家作品展，意大利羅馬
1961 八月沙龍美展，香港聖約翰副堂
1962 今日香港藝術展，香港博物美術館
第二屆香港國際沙龍美術展（亦展於 63）
香港藝術家聯展，雅苑畫廊
第一屆國際美術展，越南西貢（獲榮譽獎狀）
1963 張林聯展，香港大會堂
1964 第一屆中元畫會展，香港大會堂（亦展於 65，66，67，68，69，70）
美國匹茲堡肯納基學會國際美展
1965 東南亞美術巡迴展
西德貝魯瑟國際藝術展
1966 當代香港藝術家聯展，香港三集畫廊
1967 香港博物美術館藏品展，香港博物美術館
1968 藝術家眼中的香港，香港博物美術館
1969 雕刻模型及素描展，香港博物美術館
當代香港藝術展，香港博物美術館（亦展於 71，72，75，77）
1970 日本大阪七零年世界博覽會香港館藝術展
香港四藝術家展，香港博物美術館
1971 今日香港藝術，英國四大城市巡迴展
第二屆當代國際藝術三年展，印度新德里
1976 藝評家的選擇展，香港聖約翰救傷會總部
藝展七六，香港大學馮平山博物館（亦展於 78，81，84）
1977 第一選擇展，香港聖約翰救傷會總部（亦展於 78，79，80，82，83，84，85，86 於香港藝術中心）
香港藝術中心開幕美展
1979 香港三藝術家草圖展，香港藝術中心

Contemporary Hong Kong Art Biennial Exhibition, Hong Kong Museum of Art (also in `83, and `85)
Contemporary Art Hong Kong, Raya Gallery, Victoria, Australia

1981 Works of Contemporary Hong Kong Artists, Museum of Canton, China
Hong Kong Art 1970-80, Hong Kong Museum of Art

1982 6 Chinesen Aus Hong Kong, Galerie Henning, Hamberg, Germany
Contemporary Hong Kong Art, Metropolitan Museum of Manila, Philippines
Hong Kong Contemporary Sculpture Exhibition, Hong Kong Arts Centre

1983 10th National Arts Exhibition, Taiwan National Museum
Overseas Chinese Artists Exhibition, Taipei Fine Arts Museum, Taiwan
Museum Opening Arts Exhibition, Taipei Fine Arts Museum, Taiwan

1984 Contemporary Open Air Sculpture, Hong Kong Museum of Art
Sculpture in Hong Kong, The Goethe Institut, German Cultural Centre, Hong Kong

1985 The Sculpture Show, Exchange Square, Hong Kong

1986 Hong Kong Sculpture `86, Fung Ping Shan Museum, University of Hong Kong
Hong Kong & Overseas Chinese Artists, Canton Fine Arts Institute, China
Drawings `86--Hong Kong & New York Chinese Artists, HK Institute for Promotion of Chinese Culture

1987 Contemporary Chinese Painting, Shin Kong Life Insurance Art Gallery, Taiwan

1988 In the Dimensions--Chinese Sculpture Today, Exchange Square, Hong Kong
Ten Years of Hong Kong Sculpture, Hong Kong Arts Centre
Moderne Chinesische Kunst Aus Hong Kong, Galerie Art East Art West, Hamburg, Germany
Collection of Asia Watercolour Works, Osaka, Japan

1989 The Sculpture Walk, Kowloon Park
Hong Kong Cultural Centre Art Exhibition, Hong Kong
Hong Kong Convention and Exhibition Centre Art Exhibition, Hong Kong
Tradition and Creation, National Palace Museum, Taipei

1990 Contemporary Artists Drawing Exhibition, Cheng Pin Gallery, Taipei.

1993 Asian Art Fair, Hong Kong
Duchamp Gallery, Taiwan

1994 Asian Art Fair, Hong Kong
Taipei Fine Arts Museum Taipei, Taiwan
Crown Art Center, Taipei, Taiwan

1995 Tresors, Singapore
Art Asia Hong Kong – HK Convention & Exhibition Center
Crown Art Center, Taipei, Taiwan
Art Trends 95 – HK Convention & Exhibition Center
Faculty show of Fine Arts Department, The Chinese University of Hong Kong

1996 Tresors, Singapore
Taipei & Hong Kong Leading Artist Exhibition, Museum Annex, Hong Kong
The 11th Asian International Art Exhibition, Metropolitan Museum of Manila, Philippines

1997 Faculty show of 40th Anniversary of Fine Arts Department, The Chinese University of Hong Kong

2000 Valentine Willie, Kuala Lumpur, Malaysia

2002 Cheung Yee and Hong Kong Contemporary, iPreciation, Singapore

當代香港藝術雙年展，香港藝術館（亦展於83，85）
當代香港藝術展，澳洲維多利亞雷耶畫廊

1981 香港現代藝術家作品聯展，中國廣東省博物館
香港藝術 1970 – 80，香港藝術館

1982 香港六藝術家聯展，西德漢堡韓寧畫廊
菲律賓馬尼拉大都會博物館主辦當代香港藝術展
當代香港雕塑展，香港藝術中心

1983 第十屆全國美術展覽，台北國立藝術館
海外華僑華裔藝術家展覽，台北市立美術館
台北市立美術館開幕展，台北市立美術館

1984 當代戶外雕塑展，香港藝術館
香港雕塑，香港德國文化中心歌德學院

1985 當代中國雕塑，香港交易廣場

1986 香港雕塑八六，香港大學馮平山博物館
香港及海外華裔藝術家聯展，中國廣州美術學院
素描八六 ----- 香港及紐約中國藝術家，香港中華文化促進中心

1987 當代中國水墨畫展，台北新光人壽保險大廈畫廊

1988 現代中國雕塑展，香港交易廣場
香港十年雕塑展，香港藝術中心
香港現代中國美術展，德國漢堡東西畫廊
亞洲水彩展，日本大阪

1989 九龍公園雕塑廊
香港文化中心開幕展
香港會議展覽中心藝術展
傳統與創新，台北故宮博物院

1990 當代藝術家素描展，台北誠品畫廊

1993 亞洲藝術博覽會，香港
杜象藝術空間，高雄，台灣

1994 亞洲藝術博覽會，香港
台灣市立美術館
皇冠藝文中心，台北

1995 Tresors，星加坡
香港亞洲藝術 – 香港會議展覽中心
藝術潮流 95 –香港會議展覽中心
皇冠藝文中心，台北
大學藝術系學院展，香港中文大學

1996 Tresors，星加坡
台北及香港傑出藝術家展，藝術館別館，香港
第 11 屆亞洲國際藝術家展，菲律賓馬尼拉大都會博物館

1997 第 40 屆大學藝術系學院展，香港中文大學

2000 Valentine Willie，吉隆坡，馬來西亞

2002 張義與香港當代藝術，星加坡誰先覺

2007 2007年台北國際藝術博覽會
韓國國際藝術博覽會
藝術北京2007

2008 美國紐約Bridge ArtFair New York 2008

2007 Art Taipei 2007, Taiwan
Korea International Art Fair, Korea
Art BeiJing 2007, China
2008 Bridge ArtFair New York 2008, U.S.A.

PRINT EXHIBITIONS

1966 15th National Print Exhibition, Brooklyn Museum, New York
37th Northwest Printmakers International Exhibition, Seattle, U.S.A.
1967 Contemporary Asian Prints, City Museum and Art Gallery, Hong Kong
1969 Prints, Drawings and Ink Paintings by Hong Kong Artists, City Museum and Art Gallery, Hong Kong
1970 Mostra Internazionale della Xilografia Contemporanea, Spain
1st International Biennial Exhibition of Prints in Seoul, Korea
1971 Mostra Internazionale della Xilografia Asia Oggi, Centro D`arte Mediterranea
Xilographie d`Aujourd`hui, I.A.A.C., Paris
Mostra Internazionale della Xilografia Contemporanea, Amici dell` Arte, Faenza
1972 Exposicion Interncional De La Xilografia Contemporanea, Madrid
Mostra Internazionale Di Xilografia, Milano, Italia
1973 Contemporary Prints by Chinese Artists, Hong Kong Museum of Art
Mostra Internazionale di Xilografia Contemporanea, Milano, Italy
1974 Asia Oggi, Rassegna di Grafica Contemporanea, Milano, Italy
9th International Biennial Exhibition of Prints in Tokyo, Japan
1976 Modern Prints by Chinese Artists, Hong Kong Museum of Art
1978 International Exchange Exhibition of Prints, Seoul, Korea
6th Biennale Internazaionale Della Grafica D`Arte, Firenze, Prato
Contemporary Print Exhibition, Printmakers Art Gallery, Taiwan
1979 Contemporary Oriental Graphic Show, Miaoya Zhai Gallery, Arizona, U.S.A.
1980 Gallery Eighties Opening Exhibition, Toronto, Canada
1982 Contemporary Chinese Prints, St. John University, Jamaica, NY., U.S.A.
1983 Contemporary Hong Kong Prints, Hong Kong Museum of Art
Chinese Artists Prints Exhibition, Spring Gallery, Taiwan
1985 10th Prints Exhibition, Hong Kong Graphics Society
Hong Kong & Overseas Chinese Artists Print Exhibition
Hong Kong Institute for Promotion of Chinese Art
1986 Modern Prints Exhibition, The Chinese University of Hong Kong
1989 4th International Biennial Print Exhibition, 1989. Taipei Fine Arts Museum
1992 Macau Gravura 92 Printmaking, Macau

COMMISSIONS

1963 Hong Kong Hilton *Copper Murals*
1964 Taipei Ambassador Hotel *Bronze Murals*
1965 Hong Kong Mandarin Hotel *Copper Murals*
1966 Leo Kornblath Associates, N.Y. *Copper Murals*

版畫展

1966 第十五屆版畫展，美國紐約布魯克連博物館
第三十七屆西北版畫家國際展，美國西雅圖
1967 當代亞洲版畫展，香港博物美術館
1969 香港藝術家版畫素描水墨展，香港博物美術館
1970 當代國際木刻展，西班牙
第一屆國際版畫雙年展，韓國漢城
1971 亞州木刻展，地中海藝術中心
當代國際木刻展，法國巴黎
當代國際木刻展，意大利法恩扎
1972 當代國際木刻展，西班牙馬德里
當代國際木刻展，意大利米蘭市
1973 當代中國藝術家版畫展，香港藝術館
當代國際木刻展，意大利米蘭市
1974 當代亞洲木刻展，意大利米蘭市
第九屆國際版畫雙年展，日本東京
1976 中國藝術家現代版畫展，香港藝術館
1978 國際版畫交流展，韓國漢城
第六屆國際版畫雙年展，意大利佛羅倫斯
當代版畫展，台北版畫家畫廊
1979 當代東方版畫展，美國阿里桑那州澤爾畫廊
1980 八零年代畫廊版畫展，加拿大多倫多
1982 聖約翰大學當代中國版畫展，美國紐約
1983 當代香港版畫展，香港藝術館
中國藝術家版畫聯展，台北春之畫廊
1985 香港版畫協會十周年展，香港版畫協會
香港及海外華僑藝術家版畫展，香港中華文化促進中心
1986 現代版畫展，香港中文大學
1989 第四屆國際版畫雙年展，台灣台北市立美術館
1992 澳門版畫展

香港及海外委任作品

1963 香港希爾頓酒店金屬浮雕壁畫
1964 台北國賓酒店青銅壁畫
1965 香港文華酒店銅壁畫
1966 美國紐約李奧龔伯建築師公司銅壁畫
1968 香港王歐陽建築師公司銅壁畫
1969 香港希爾頓酒店不銹鋼壁畫及木雕壁畫
香港中文大學校外進修部金屬壁畫
台北萬國寶通銀行金屬壁畫
菲律賓馬尼拉生力啤酒廠金屬壁畫
馬尼拉菲律賓商業銀行金屬壁畫及木雕壁畫
1970 泰國曼谷喜來登酒店銅壁畫
菲律賓馬尼拉洛辛大廈金屬壁畫
美國紐約梅勒公司金屬壁畫
1971 香港商業電台青銅壁畫
香港王董建築師公司金屬壁畫
美國紐約米勒供應公司金屬壁畫
1972 香港匯豐銀行金屬壁畫
關島希爾頓酒店金屬壁畫
香港卡嘉公司木雕壁畫
美國凱悅酒店集團金屬壁畫及花崗石雕

1968 Wong & Ouyang & Associates *Copper Murals*

1969 Hong Kong Hilton *Metal & Wooden Murals*
Extramural Dept., Chinese University *Metal Mural*
First National City Bank, Taipei *Metal Mural*
San Miguel, Manila *Metal Mural*
Philippine Bank of Commerce, Manila *Wooden & Metal Murals*

1970 Locsin Bldg., Manila *Metal Murals*
Sheraton Hotel, Bangkok *Metal Murals*
The Miller Organization Inc., N.Y. *Metal Murals*

1971 Commercial Radio, Hong Kong *Metal Mural*
Wong Tung & Partners, Hong Kong *Metal Murals*
Miller Supply Corp., N.Y. *Metal Murals*

1972 Hong Kong & Shanghai Banking Corporation, Hong Kong *Metal Murals*
Hilton Hotel, Guam *Metal Murals*
W.I. Carr, Hong Kong *Wooden Murals*
Hyatt Corp., U.S.A. *Granite Sculptures & Metal Murals*

1973 Shanghai Commercial Bank, Hong Kong *Concrete Murals*
Sheraton Hotel, Hong Kong *Copper, Bronze & Wooden Murals, Marble Sculptures, Lift Doors & Cast Paper Prints*
Manila Bankers Life Insurance Corp. *Metal Mural*

1974 Hayashida Hotel, Kagoshima, Japan *Wooden Sculpture & Metal Murals*
Park Hotel, Hong Kong *Cast Paper Mural*
Bancom International Ltd., Hong Kong *Cast Paper Mural*

1975 Ralli (HK) Ltd., Hong Kong *Metal Mural*
The Bank of Canton Ltd., Hong Kong *Metal Mural*
Wing Hang Bank, Hong Kong *Metal Mural*

1976 Plaza Hotel, Hong Kong *Wooden Murals*
Citibank Tower, Hong Kong *Wooden Murals*
Hsin Yieh Architect & Associates, Hong Kong *Metal Murals*
Sheraton Hotel, Hong Kong *Cast Paper Prints*

1977 Sheraton-Molokai Hotel, Hawaii *Metal Murals*
Manufacturers Hanover Trust Co., Hong Kong *Wooden & Metal Murals, Cast Paper Prints*
American Express, Hong Kong *Cast Paper Murals*

1978 The Hong Kong & Shanghai Banking Corporation, Hong Kong *Wooden Murals*
China Building, Hong Kong *Stainless Steel Murals*
The Commercial Bank of Hong Kong Ltd. *Wooden & Metal Murals*

1979 Gloucester Tower, Landmark, Hong Kong *Cast Bronze Mural*
Grindlays Dao Heng Bank Ltd., Hong Kong *Paper Prints*
Hong Kong Telephone *Paper Prints*

1973 香港上海商業銀行水泥壁畫
香港喜來登酒店金屬壁畫、木雕壁畫、大理石雕、銅門及鑄紙版畫
菲律賓馬尼拉銀行家人壽保險公司金屬壁畫

1974 日本鹿兒島酒店金屬壁畫及木雕
香港百樂酒店鑄紙壁畫
香港國際商業銀行鑄紙壁畫

1975 香港萊利棉花公司金屬壁畫
香港廣東銀行金屬壁畫
香港永亨銀行金屬壁畫

1976 香港華都酒店木雕壁畫
香港萬國寶通銀行木雕壁畫
香港興業建築師公司金屬壁畫
香港喜來登酒店鑄紙版畫

1977 美國夏威夷喜來登酒店銅壁畫
香港漢諾華信託公司金屬壁畫、木雕壁畫及鑄紙版畫
香港美國運通銀行鑄紙壁畫

1978 香港匯豐銀行木雕壁畫
香港華人行大廈不銹鋼壁畫
香港商業銀行木雕壁畫及金屬壁畫

1979 香港置地廣場青銅鑄造壁畫
香港道亨銀行鑄紙版畫
香港電話公司鑄紙版畫
香港電力公司木雕壁畫

1980 美國阿里桑那州鳳凰城好彩集團金屬壁畫及鑄紙壁畫
香港新九龍半島中心戶外水泥壁畫

1981 香港可口可樂公司金屬壁畫
香港馬可孛羅酒店鑄紙版畫

1983 香港東亞銀行大堂木雕壁畫

1984 香港九龍會鑄紙壁畫
香港富麗華酒店木雕壁畫

1985 香港九龍東尖沙咀公園水池鑄銅雕刻（市政局）
香港新界沙田馬會鑄紙壁畫及金屬壁畫
香港海港酒店鑄紙壁畫

1987 香港瑞士銀行鑄紙版畫

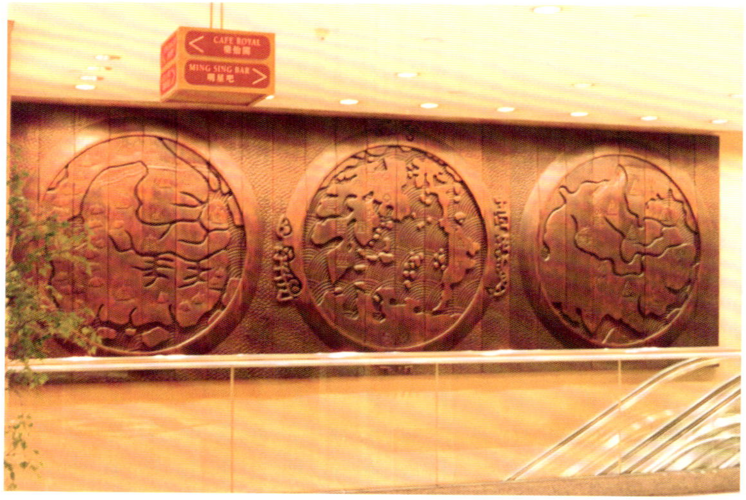

1984 Furama Hotel, Hong Kong

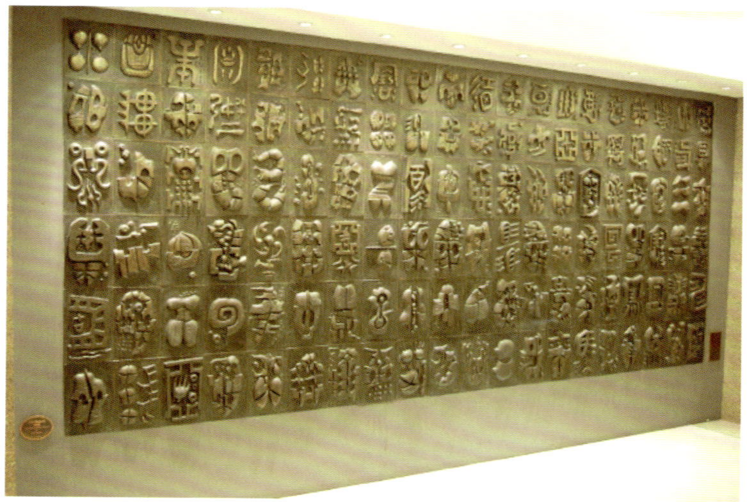

1979 Gloucester Tower, Landmark, Hong Kong; 1999 Citylink, Singapore

	Hong Kong Electric Co. Ltd. *Wooden Mural*
1980	Lucky Stores Inc., Phoenix, Arizona, U.S.A. *Metal & Paper Murals*
	Peninsula Centre, Hong Kong *Cast Concrete Murals*
1981	Coca Cola, Hong Kong *Metal Mural*
	The Marco Polo, Hong Kong *Cast Paper Prints*
1983	East Asia Bank, Hong Kong *Wooden Mural*
1984	Kowloon Club, Hong Kong *Cast Paper Murals*
	Furama Hotel, Hong Kong *Wooden Murals*
1985	East Kowloon Park, Hong Kong *Bronze Sculpture*
	Jockey Club, Shatin, N.T., Hong Kong *Metal & Paper Murals*
	Victoria Hotel, Hong Kong *Cast Paper Murals*
1987	Swiss Bank Corp., Hong Kong *Cast Paper Prints*
1988	Princes Building, Hong Kong *Wooden Mural*
	Grand Plaza Hotel, Hong Kong *Cast Paper Murals*
1989	Hong Kong Cultural Centre *Wooden Murals*
	Hong Kong Convention and Exhibition Centre *Wooden Murals*
2003	Taipei 101, Taiwan *Bronze Murals*

1988	香港太子行大廈木浮雕壁畫
	香港格蘭酒店鑄紙壁畫
1989	香港文化中心大堂木雕壁畫
	香港會議展覽中心木雕壁畫
2003	台灣台北 101 銅壁畫

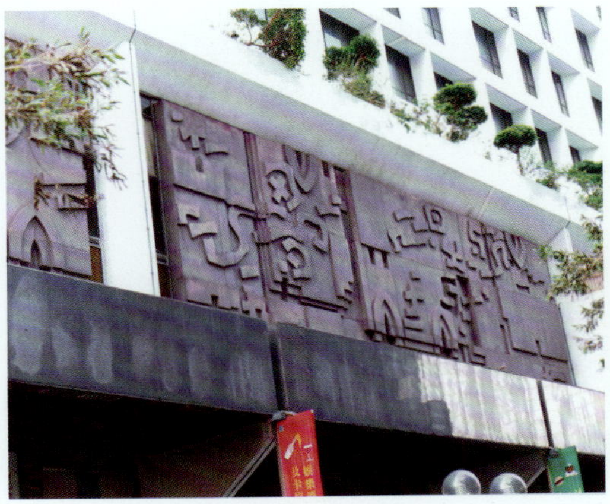
1980 Peninsula Centre, Hong Kong

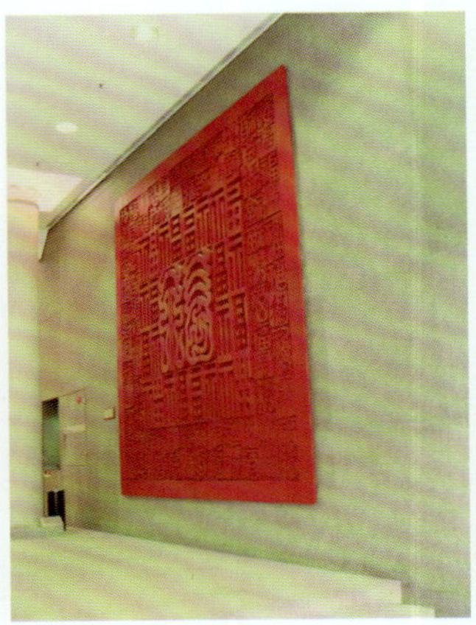
1983 East Asia Bank, Hong Kong

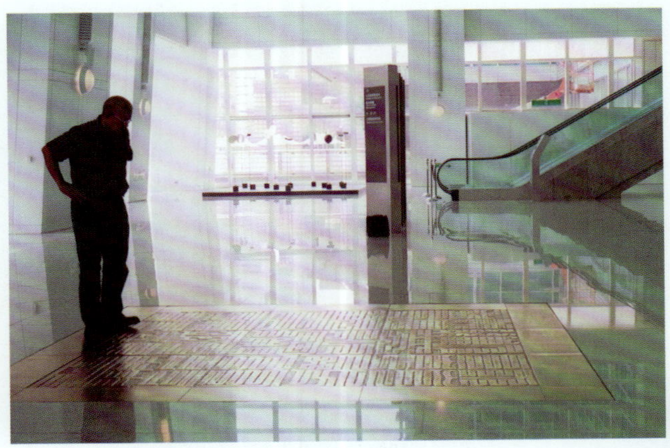
2004 Taipei 101, Taiwan

APPENDIX

Sculpture 雕塑 1964 - 2007

DOOR
門
Bronze
112 x 112 cm
1964
Pg. 15

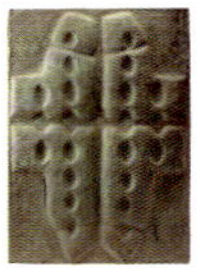

FORTUNE
福
Bronze
113 x 77 cm
1964
Pg. 16

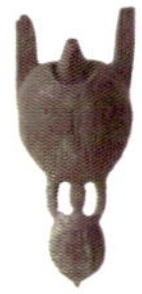

MOTHER & CHILD
母子
Bronze
34 x 15 cm
1964
Pg. 17

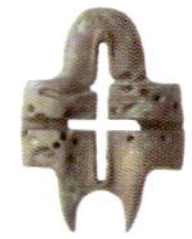

FORTUNE
卜
Bronze
31 x 22 cm
1968
Pg. 18

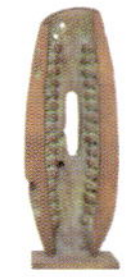

FEMALE
坤儀
Bronze
30 x 10 x 9 cm
1968
Pg. 19

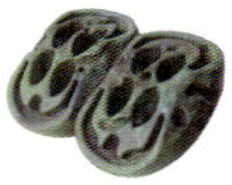

TWINS
連理
Bronze
14.5 x 28 x 25 cm
1970
Pg. 20

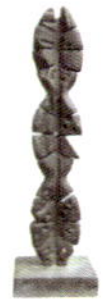

THREE SPIRIT
三奇
Bronze
208 x 55 x 55 cm
1970
Pg. 21

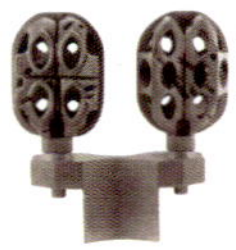

SPIRIT C D
靈丙與丁
Wood/Bronze
75 x 55 cm
1976
Pg. 22

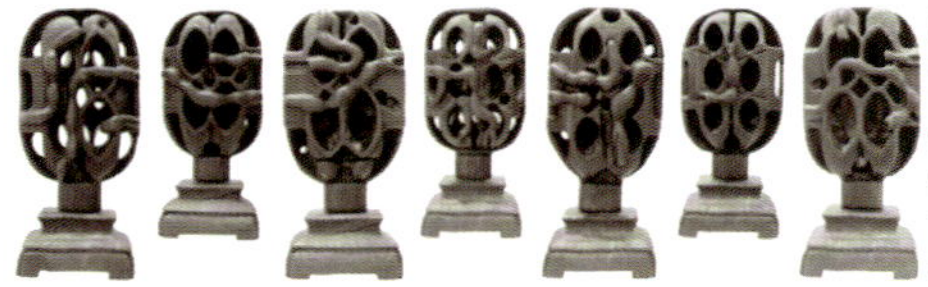

SPIRIT A - G
靈 甲-庚
Bronze
H: 45 cm
1977
Pg. 23

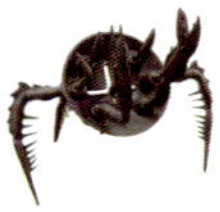

CRAB #4
跋扈將軍#四
Bronze
45 x 59 x 57 cm
1985
Pg. 24

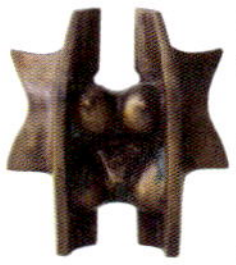

BIRD MAN #1
玄鳥 #一
Bronze
15 x 14 x 6.5 cm
1988
Pg. 25

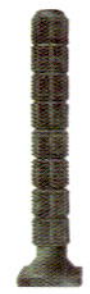

HEAVEN & EARTH
通天
Bronze
34 x 7.5 x 7.5 cm
1992
Pg. 26

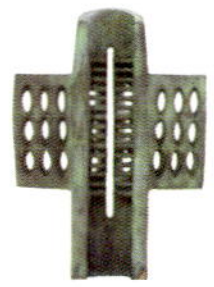

FLYING
翔
Bronze
29 x 19 x 5.5 cm
1992
Pg. 27

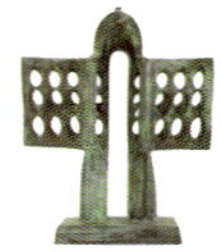

EAGLEMAN
隼人
Bronze
31 x 25 x 11 cm
1992
Pg. 28

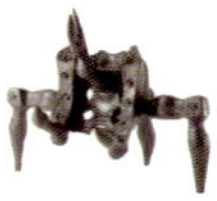

CRAB #5
伏波將軍
Bronze
68 x 65 x 87 cm
1993
Pg. 29

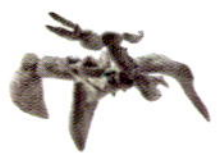

CRAB #6
老驥（橫行萬里）
Wood/Bronze
101 x 110x 162 cm
1993
Pg. 30

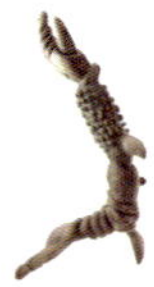

ARMSTRONG
鐵臂
Bronze
H: 83 cm
1993
Pg. 31

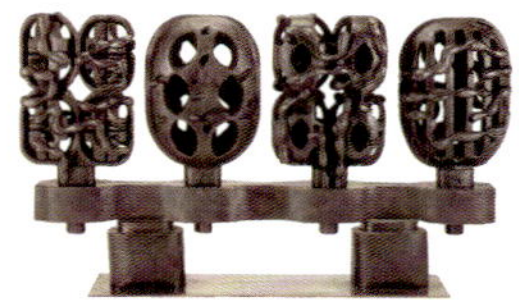

FOUR SPIRIT
四護院
Bronze
74 x 127 x 25 cm
1993
Pg. 32

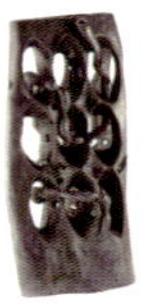

MAGIC NINE
九宮變幻
Bronze
78 x 36 cm
1993
Pg. 33

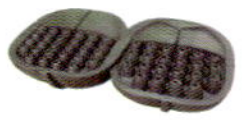

TWINS
連理
Wood
23 x 94 x 52 cm
2007
Pg. 34

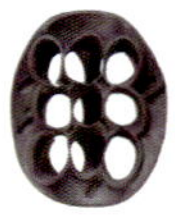

FORTUNE
福
Wood
38 x 51 x 26 cm
1975
Pg. 35

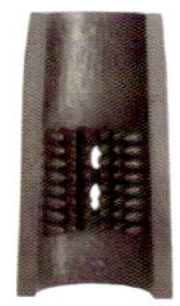

MONOLITH
祖
Wood
54.7 x 29.3 x 15.3 cm
2007
Pg. 36

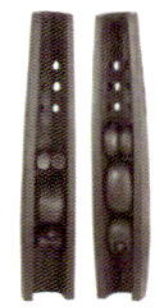

COUPLE
乾坤
Wood
117 x 20.5 x 20.5 cm
2007
Pg. 37

Wood Relief 木浮雕 1975 - 2007

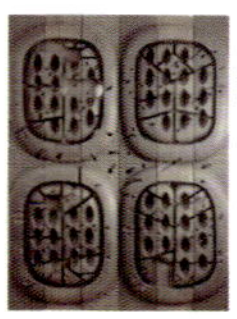

FOUR SPIRITS(FRONT)
四靈（正）
Wood Relief
264 x 183 cm
1975
Pg. 39

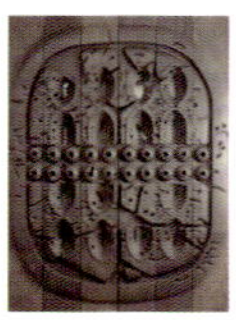

FOUR SPIRITS(BACK)
四靈（背）
Wood Relief
264 x 183 cm
1975
Pg. 40

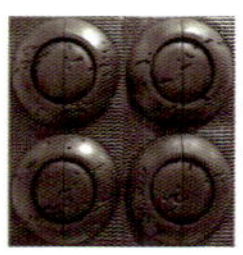

EARTH
大地
Wood Relief
122 x 122 x 10 cm
1998
Pg. 41

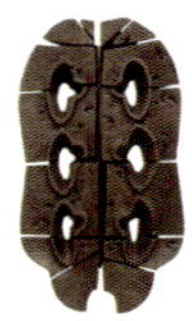

FORTUNE
富
Wood Relief
108 x 60 x 10 cm
2006
Pg. 42

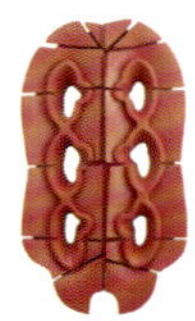

FORTUNE SIX
六合
Wood Relief
108 x 60 x 10 cm
2007
Pg. 43

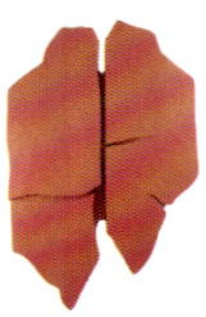

FORTUNE
福
Wood Relief
104 x 81 x 7.5 cm
2007
Pg. 44

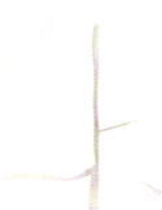

FORTUNE
福
Wood Relief
104 x 81 x 7.5 cm
2007
Pg. 45

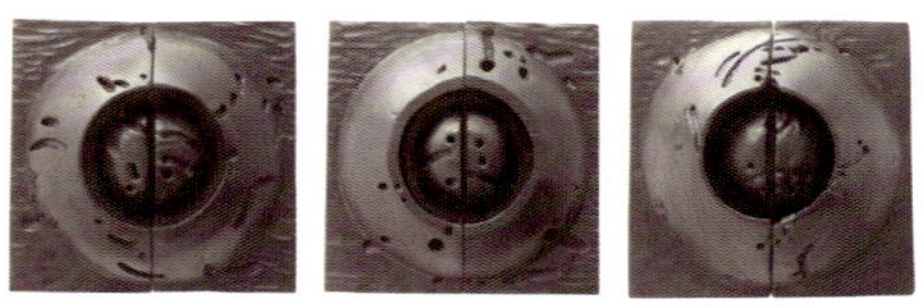

CIRCLE # 1 2 3
圓 # 一 二 三
Wood Relief
#1, 2: 29 x 29 x 7cm
#3: 31 x 31 x 11 cm
2007
Pg. 46

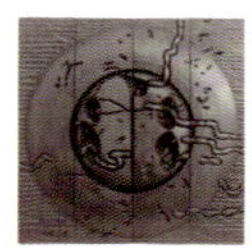

GENESIS
原
Wood Relief
122 x 122 x 10 cm
2007
Pg. 47

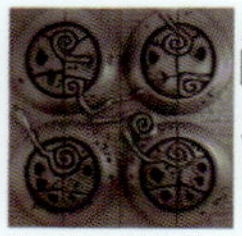

FOUR CIRCLES
四宮
Wood Relief
122 x 122 x 10 cm
2007
Pg. 48

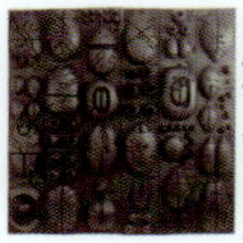

TABLET
銘
Wood Relief
183 x 183 x 15 cm
2007
Pg. 49

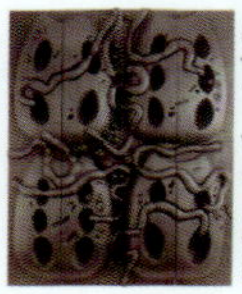

FORTUNE FOUR
方福
Wood Relief
152 x 122 x 15 cm
2007
Pg. 50

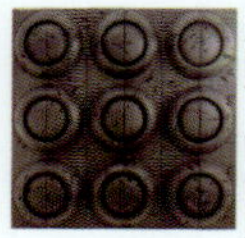

MAGIC SQUARE
九宮
Wood Relief
183 x 183 x 15 cm
2007
Pg. 51

Cast Paper 鑄紙 1995 - 2007

951128 FORTUNE 4
富
Cast Paper on Wood
92 x 91 cm
1995
Pg. 53

030319 TWIN FORTUNE
雙福
Cast Paper on Wood
48 x 53 cm
1999
Pg. 54

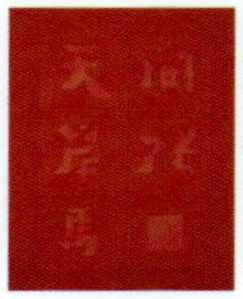

990728 SKY HORSE
天岸馬
Cast Paper on Wood
91 x 71 cm
1999
Pg. 55

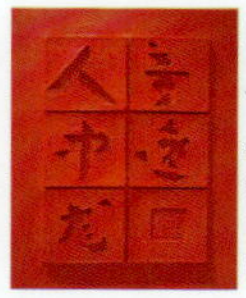

990712 DRAGON
人中龍
Cast Paper on Wood
92 x 71.5 cm
1999
Pg. 56

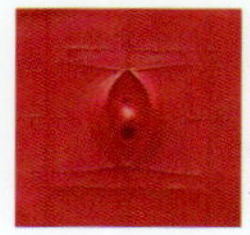

00218 BIRTH
生
Cast Paper in Frame
41 x 41 cm
1999
Pg. 57

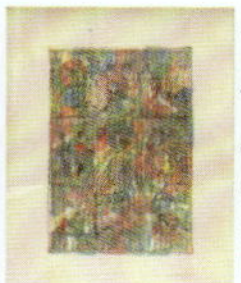

0209 FORTUNE 9
久富
Cast Paper on Wood
66 x 51 cm
2000
Pg. 58

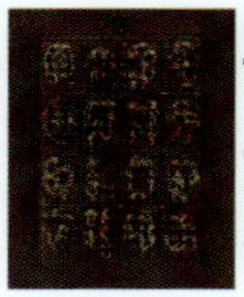

010212 FORTUNE 16
富孖八
Cast Paper on Wood
92 x 72 cm
2001
Pg. 59

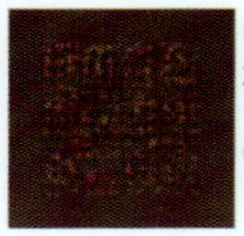

010223 FORTUNE 12
福滿年
Cast Paper on Wood
76.5 x 76.5 cm
2001
Pg. 60

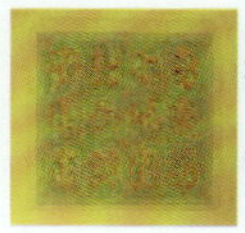

010318 FORTUNE 12
福滿年
Cast Paper on Wood
77 x 77 cm
2001
Pg. 61

020319 MING
明
Cast Paper on Wood
76 x 76 cm
2002
Pg. 62

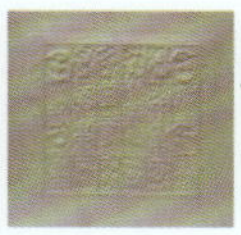

020323 HAPPY THREE
喜兆三多
Cast Paper on Wood
92 x 91 cm
2002
Pg. 63

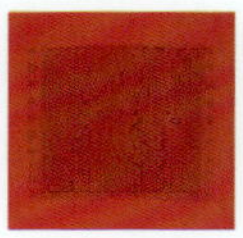

031202 CLIFF
赤壁
Cast Paper on Wood
92 x 92 cm
2003
Pg. 64

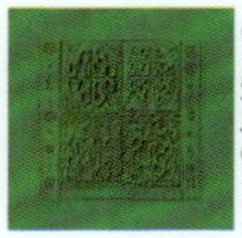

031228 TWIN FORTUNE
雙福
Cast Paper on Wood
77 x 77 cm
2003
Pg. 65

040320 POEM
詩
Cast Paper on Wood
122 x 122 cm
2004
Pg. 66

FORTUNE 50 040503
福
Cast Paper on Wood
101 x 132 cm
2004
Pg. 67

MORE HAPPY 041129
喜兆三多多
Cast Paper on Wood
100 x 130 cm
2004
Pg. 68

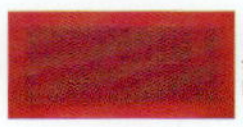

POEM 041208
詩
Cast Paper on Wood
92 x 183 cm
2005
Pg. 69

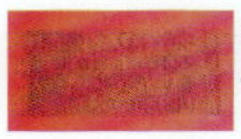

HAPPY THREE 50212
喜兆
Cast Paper on Wood
91.5 x 183.5 cm
2005
Pg. 70

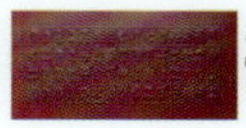

FORTUNE 50213
富
Cast Paper on Wood
91.5 x 183 cm
2005
Pg. 71

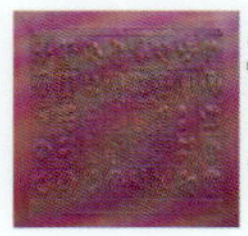

FORTUNE 50220
富
Cast Paper on Wood
122.5 x 122 cm
2005
Pg. 72

MING 50301
明
Cast Paper on Wood
92 x 92 cm
2005
Pg. 73

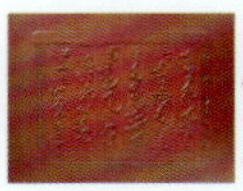

HEART MOVE 50309
心動了
Cast Paper on Wood
102 x 133 cm
2005
Pg. 74

HEART 50311
心動
Cast Paper on Wood
91.5 x 91.5 cm
2005
Pg. 75

50803 HEART MOVING
心動了
Cast Paper on Wood
92 x 183 cm
2005
Pg. 76

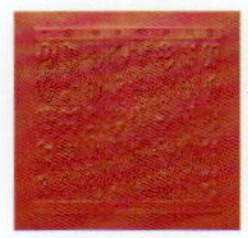

BIG FORTUNE 070101
大福
Cast Paper on Wood
121 x 122.5 cm
2007
Pg. 77

BIG FORTUNE 070102
大福
Cast Paper on Wood
122 x 122 cm
2007
Pg. 78

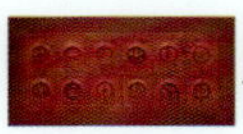

12 CIRCLES 070303
十二圓
Cast Paper on Wood
91.4 x 182.9 cm
2007
Pg. 79

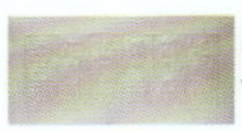

FORTUNE 12 073219
十二生肖
Cast Paper on Wood
92 x 183 cm
2007
Pg. 80

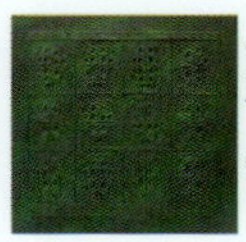

FORTUNE 12 070322
大福十二
Cast Paper on Wood
122 x 122 cm
2007
Pg. 81

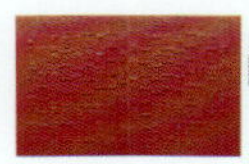

MING 070707
明
Cast Paper on Wood
132 x 203 cm (Diptych)
2007
Pg. 82

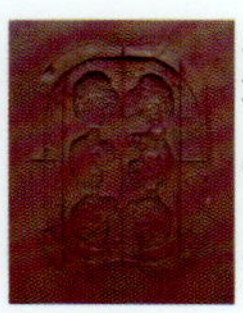

SPIRIT F 070323
坤
Cast Paper on Wood
132 x 102 cm
2007
Pg. 83

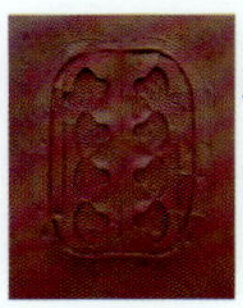

SPIRIT M 070328
乾
Cast Paper on Wood
132 x 102 cm
2007
Pg. 84